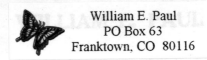

D0731481

IS THE NEW TESTAMENT RELIABLE?

A Look at the Historical Evidence

PAUL BARNETT

INTERVARSITY PRESS
DOWNERS GROVE, ILLINOIS 60515

© Paul W. Barnett, 1986

Published in the United States of America by InterVarsity Press, Downers Grove, Illinois, with permission from Hodder & Stoughton, Australia.

InterVarsity Press® is the book-publishing division of InterVarsity Christian Fellowship®, a student movement active on campus at hundreds of universities, colleges and schools of nursing in the United States of America, and a member movement of the International Fellowship of Evangelical Students. For information about local and regional activities, write Public Relations Dept., InterVarsity Christian Fellowship, 6400 Schroeder Rd., P.O. Box 7895, Madison, WI 53707-7895.

Scripture quotations, unless otherwise noted, are from the Revised Standard Version of the Bible, copyright 1946, 1952, 1971 by the Division of Christian Education of the National Council of the Churches of Christ in the U.S.A. and are used by permission.

Cover photo: Scala/Art Resource, N.Y.

ISBN 0-8308-1834-0

Printed in the United States of America ∞

Library of Congress Cataloging-in-Publication Data

Barnett, Paul (Paul William)
   [Is the New Testament history]
   Is the New Testament reliable?: a look at the historical evidence
/Paul Barnett.
     p.   cm.
   Originally published: Is the New Testament history? Sydney:
Hodder & Stoughton, 1986.
   Includes bibliographical references.
   ISBN 0-8308-1834-0
   1. Bible. N.T.—Evidences, authority, etc. 2. Bible. N.T.—
History of Biblical events. I. Title.
BS2332.B377   1992
225.9'5—dc20   92-34570
                                  CIP

16	15	14	13	12	11	10	9	8	7	6	5	4	3	2	1
06	05	04	03	02	01	00	99	98	97	96	95	94	93		

Foreword _____ 7

1 The Question of Truth _____ 9

2 Did Jesus Exist? Early Non-Christian References _____ 16

3 Fixing the Time-Frame _____ 33

4 Is the Transmission Trustworthy? _____ 43

5 The Two Witnesses _____ 49

6 Witness One: The Disciple Whom Jesus Loved _____ 56

7 Witness Two: Peter Through Mark _____ 81

8 Luke and Matthew _____ 99

9 Miracles and the Modern World _____ 111

10 The Birth of Jesus _____ 117

11 Paul and the Historical Jesus _____ 125

12 The Acts of the Apostles _____ 137

13 Is the New Testament Historically Reliable? _____ 155

14 Who Is Jesus? _____ 168

Foreword

The New Testament documents have aroused greater interest than any other writings in human history and have been studied more intensively, both in the broad sweep of their message and in the minutest details of their composition. They are so central to the claims of Christianity that the question which forms the title of this book becomes an urgent one for any serious enquirer. I recall hearing an address by C. S. Lewis one evening in the dining hall of Balliol College, Oxford, in which he argued—with the most powerful persuasion—that any student who valued his integrity, no matter what his area of study, was obliged to enquire earnestly into the truth or falsity of the Christian faith.

But this book is written in a style that will appeal to far more than students. It will attract readers young and old because its author, Dr Paul Barnett, is not only well qualified to write on the historical credibility of the New Testament but has arranged his subject matter in a clear and logical order. He approaches the documents with a refreshing openness and an awareness of the questions modern enquirers are most likely to ask. He has compressed into a modest space a remarkable amount of information about the evidence from within the New Testament and from outside, in the history and literature of the first century world. He has wisely asked the important questions about what "history" writing meant in that period, about the exceptional nature of the four gospels, about the evidence for the life and mission of Jesus and those followers whose witness to him was crucial to his claims.

Dr Barnett firmly states that he has not written a theological work, but he has surely laid the foundations on which any theological understanding of the New Testament must be built. He has included, but not obtrusively, some of his own experience as an enquirer and then one who became committed to the truth of the Christian faith and to Jesus himself. This is the ultimate question which the New Testament poses to us all.

I commend this book strongly. It is an important contribution to the Christian Beliefs Series, of which its author is also Editor.

BRUCE HARRIS
Associate Professor of History,
Macquarie University
Sydney.

CHAPTER ONE

The Question of Truth

In the year AD 135 after a three-year war, the Romans captured and beheaded the leader of a major Jewish uprising in which more than half a million Jews were killed, fifty fortresses destroyed and almost a thousand villages razed. This man, who called himself "President of Israel" and issued coins and land deeds as such, was hailed as the Messiah by the leading rabbi of the day. A formidable generalissimo who amputated a finger from each serving soldier, he was only removed, according to the Roman Emperor Hadrian, by an "act of God". And yet, though this man was so great a figure, little evidence from the period has come to us, and such as there is does not even accurately record his name. His real name, ben Kosiba, has only been known outside his own generation since 1951, when some personal letters were discovered in a cave near the Dead Sea.

Almost exactly a century before ben Kosiba, the Romans had executed another Jew who had also been active in public for about three years. He had only twelve close followers and he neither minted coins nor issued land deeds. But within a generation after his death his name was known outside Palestine, and within three centuries, his symbol was inscribed on the shields of the soldiers of the Roman Emperor Constantine and also on his coinage. Few parts of the world today have not heard the name of Jesus, if only in blasphemy! Millions of people claim to be his followers. Ben Kosiba and Jesus—quite a contrast, and one to which we shall return.

This book is written for people with questions about the historical reliability of the New Testament—questions like:

How close in time are the documents to Jesus?

Can we believe the writings of the "biased" early Christians?

Were any of the writers of the New Testament books eye-witnesses?

Can we know if what was originally written has escaped alteration down through the centuries?

Do we have any information apart from Christian sources?

This book is addressed to these and related questions.

Three important preliminaries
First, please notice that our subject is not the *theological* but the *historical* reliability of the New Testament. These two aspects of reliability dovetail together into one total concept of reliability. They are really inseparable since the theology of the New Testament depends on the events concerning Jesus having actually taken place and the events concerning Jesus are themselves profoundly theological. Nevertheless, this book will concentrate on the historical question.

Since the emphasis will be on history, on events, our area of investigation will be limited to the gospels, the Acts of the Apostles and the relatively few autobiographical or historical sections of Paul's letters.

If the gospels and Acts are historical as well as theological, how historical are they?

Like other historical work in the ancient world, the gospels and Acts differ from the writing of twentieth century historians which is immensely detailed, with each statement supported by a reference. It would be unfair, however, to reject ancient histories like the gospels and Acts, because they do not conform to modern conventions of history writing. The writers of the gospels and Acts supply facts, many facts, but not as comprehensively or elaborately as some modern authors do. The biblical history writers have given their readers sufficient evidence on which to base a valid response to Jesus; but it probably isn't possible, from the information they have given, to rewrite the gospels and Acts as precise modern histories. This, however, would be an unreasonable demand and one that could not be fairly made of Josephus or Tacitus or any other historical writer of the same period. While, as we have stated, the New Testament does not assume the form of a history or a biography, being primarily concerned with Christian beliefs and behavior, it does nevertheless rest on a foundation of facts. Many historical and biographical details are supplied which allow the historian to make a reasonable and coherent reconstruction, even if it is not complete in every respect. We may take it that the historical information contained in the New Testament is at least as accurate as that in other sources of the same period upon which modern historians depend when writing biographies of, say, Julius Caesar or King Herod the Great.

It may come as a surprise to us to know how professional many writers of that age were, even though they lacked modern tools such as computers and good maps. Those authors, including New Testament authors, certainly knew the difference between history and legend.[1] It would be utterly fallacious to believe, for example, that the New Testament story about King Herod the Great was like the story of King Arthur. Because of the extent, soberness, diversity and basic agreement of the available sources of information, the account of Herod can be accepted with considerable confidence. On the other hand, the information about Arthur, comes from legends and romantic stories and in so many differing versions as to make the very existence of Arthur doubtful. The information we have about Jesus, Peter and Paul was recorded close in time to the events related and is sufficiently confirmed for the historicity of Jesus, Peter and Paul to be put in the same general class as, for example, that of Caesar or Herod

Second, what I have to say about the historical accuracy of the New Testament, does not require the reader's acceptance of it as part of the inspired word of God. That is a view you may come to, as I have However, it would be unreasonable to expect the as yet unconvinced reader to adopt this belief, nor is it my intention here to argue that case, which is a question of theology.[2] When you have finished this book you may say that you now believe that the documents of the New Testament have a definite historical aspect, and that they are essentially reliable. I do not expect you to say that you now believe it is the word of God, and therefore will confine my comments to those matters which can be checked as historical fact, or for which a case of probability can be argued. You will not be expected to accept anything in this book "by faith". What I will attempt to present is an objectively reasoned case, the details of which will be open to further inquiry.

Third, it will be helpful if we also keep in mind the fact that what is now called the New Testament, originally consisted of twenty-seven separate scrolls of varying length. Matthew, for example, would have been written on a papyrus scroll ten metres long. Those twenty-seven scrolls were written by: Matthew; Mark; Luke (Gospel and Acts); John (Gospel, Letters, perhaps Revelation); Paul; the author of Hebrews; James; Peter and Jude— nine authors in all, ten if Revelation was by a different John. It is vital to understand that most of the authors wrote independently of one another, and that their scrolls circulated separately until the second century.

With the passage of time and the growth of new congregations, the copies of the original scrolls were gathered together for reading in church. Although Christian writers of the second and third century list the documents which were in use in the churches, the list of books of the New Testament as we have them today, was not formalised until late in the fourth century by the Councils of Hippo Regius and Carthage in North Africa. F.F. Bruce comments that: "what these [ecclesiastical] councils did was not to impose something new upon the Christian communities but to codify what was already the general practice of those communities".[3]

A major obstacle

But how sure can we be about people and events so long ago? To many people this is a major obstacle barring the path to further enquiry about Jesus. Why couldn't he have lived closer to our own time?

Two comments may be offered.

Part of the difficulty is a mathematical illusion. Two thousand years seems such a vast expanse of time. But what if we measured the period since the birth of Jesus by individual life spans? If we take the average life-span to be about seventy years, it would require no more than thirty such life-spans to bring us back to New Testament times. The first would take us to the 1914–18 war, the second into Queen Victoria's era, the third to the Napoleonic wars and so on. The thirtieth would take us to the birth of Jesus. Measured in years the two thousand year period is hard to comprehend, but not in terms of individual life spans.

Another problem for us is to think of history in neat progressive terms. Old means primitive; recent means developed. While this may be true of history overall, it is by no means true that the tenth century is an exact mid-point in terms of "progress" between Jesus in the first century and our generation in the twentieth. In many ways the first century, when Graeco–Roman society was at its height, was more civilized than the Middle or

"Dark" Ages. In fact, we know more about the Roman emperor Augustus than about the eleventh century English king Harold, even though the latter is a thousand years closer to us than the former. It is fortunate for the study of Christian origins that Jesus was born in such a literate, well-documented period.

Let me conclude this chapter on a personal note. What I found compelling about Christianity as a young adult was the sense of gratitude associated with the forgiveness of sins through the death of Christ. Christianity was "true" for me in a personal way and I accepted it was as true objectively or historically as my new Christian friends assured me it was, but without real confidence.

Some time later I entered theological college to train for the ministry. While some attention was given to questions of history and truth, most of my time there was devoted to the study of Greek and Hebrew, the intensive exegesis of the literature of the Bible and to systematic theology. A good foundation of theological knowledge was laid, but the history question was (for me) still up in the air.

It was only later, when I studied ancient history at university, that the matter was finally settled in my mind. In the course of three years of Roman and Greek history and Greek language I came to appreciate how solid the evidence for Christianity was, relative to other great people and movements in antiquity. It wasn't that our courses investigated Christianity, quite the reverse. In fact, Jesus was only once or twice referred to in the many lectures on ancient history I attended at university. What I discovered was that the historical evidence for Jesus and the origins of Christianity compared favourably with that available for Tiberius, the Roman emperor in whose time Jesus exercised his ministry or for Alexander the Great or the emperor Nero.

This book is written from the conviction that there is

a sound historical basis to the New Testament. What it attempts to do is to place the evidence before the reader for his examination. Let the evidence speak for itself and lead where it will.

Further reading to Chapter One:
C.H. Dodd, *The Founder of Christianity*, Collins, London, 1971.
D. Winter, *The Search for the Real Jesus*, Hodder and Stoughton, London, 1982.
Y. Yadin, *Bar-Kochba*, Weidenfeld and Nicolson, London, 1978.

Notes
[1]*See*, for example, 2 Peter 1:16, "We did not follow cleverly devised myths..."

[2]*See*, I.H. Marshall, *Biblical Inspiration*, Hodder & Stoughton, London, 1982.

[3]F.F. Bruce, *The New Testament Documents*, I.V.P. London, 1963.

CHAPTER TWO

Did Jesus Exist? Early Non-Christian References

As we have seen, the book we call the New Testament is a slim collection of writings made up of twenty-seven pieces of varying length written by nine or ten different authors, all of them convinced Christians.

That's fine if you are already a Christian. But what if you're not? Are you expected to make up your mind about Jesus just on the "say-so" of nine or ten biased Christians who wrote the New Testament? It would be rather like having to reach a decision about Karl Marx based entirely on what Marxists say about him.

And what if Jesus never existed anyway? Many people have wondered about that, and the thought has crossed my own mind more than once. Perhaps he was a figment of the imagination of those early Christians? This opinion has been expressed periodically in a serious way, most recently by G. Wells, a professor of German who in 1971 wrote a book entitled *The Jesus of the Early Christians*.

Despite their admitted bias, I hope to show that the New Testament writers themselves are the best reason for believing about the existence of Jesus. However, as it happens, there is other early information about Jesus written by non-Christians. These non-Christian sources fall into two broad classes, Roman and Jewish.

ROMAN SOURCES

Pliny: letters from Bithynia c. AD 112

In about AD 110 the Emperor Trajan sent Pliny (AD 61–113), an experienced administrator, as governor of the disorderly province of Bithynia, south of the Black Sea. A few years later Pliny wrote to the emperor seeking advice about a troublesome group known as "Christians". An unsigned paper giving the names of many Christians had been given to the governor, who had forthwith put them in prison. But how was he to conduct the trial? What punishments were appropriate? Should the young be punished as severely as the old? Would renunciation of Jesus earn pardon? Pliny wrote to the Emperor Trajan for advice on these and similar questions.

The Christian movement had taken quite a hold in the region. Pliny complained to Trajan that *"many* of all ages and every rank and also of both sexes" were involved, and that like a spreading disease "not the cities only, but also the villages and the country" were affected. So powerful had the new movement become that the temples had become deserted and those who sold food for the animal sacrifices had not been able to find buyers. Pliny's letter reveals that this movement was not altogether new, since some of the prisoners whom he threatened said that they had given up being Christians twenty years earlier. We conclude that there must have been Christians in Bithynia at least by the late eighties of the first century AD, perhaps earlier. Peter's first letter, written in the early sixties, is addressed to Christians in Bithynia (among others) thus confirming what we learn from Pliny.

Who were these "Christians" and what did they believe? Pliny interrogated them and told Trajan:

They maintained, however, that the amount of their fault or error had been this, that it was their habit on a fixed day to assemble before daylight and recite by turns a form of words to Christ as a god; and that they bound themselves with an oath, not for any crime, but not to commit theft or robbery or adultery, not to break their word, and not to deny a deposit when demanded. After this was done, their custom was to depart, and to meet again to take food, but ordinary and harmless food.[1]

Pliny's comments are the earliest surviving non-Christian description of what Christians believed and how they lived. What is of greatest interest is that these people regarded Christ as a god (or as God). They did not venerate him as a deceased martyr but agreed together by a form of words that he was a divine figure, in some way their living contemporary.

There is no reason to believe that their attitude to Jesus was a recent development. Half a century earlier Peter had reminded the Christians of Bithynia (and others) that, "Through him [that is, Christ] you believed in God, who raised him from the dead and glorified him..." (1 Peter 1:21).

Without knowing it, Pliny confirms as historically accurate some details found in the New Testament.

First, he confirms that early Christianity sometimes destroyed the business side of the older religions. Like the shrine makers in Ephesus (Acts 19:24ff) the suppliers of food for sacrifical animals in Bithynia were put out of business by the impact of the Christian movement.

Second, Pliny mentions that Christians met for worship on a "fixed day". This can be compared with the meeting in Troas on the "first day of the week" to "break bread" (Acts 20:7) which probably refers to the Holy Communion.

Third, Pliny states that the Christians prayed to Jesus as God (or as a god) while refusing to curse him. This confirms as accurate Paul's statement that "no one speaking by the Spirit of God ever says 'Jesus be cursed!' and no one can say 'Jesus is Lord' except by the Holy Spirit" (1 Corinthians 12:3).

This encourages us to believe, at least in these three references, that the biblical account is true.

Based on what Pliny wrote there can be no doubt about the existence in about AD 110 of a substantial body of Christians in remote Bithynia. This is a fact of history. But how do we explain this fact? How did they come to be there? Their presence was an historical *effect* for which there was some *cause*. What was it?

Christian inscription in Pompeii

```
R O T A S
O P E R A
T E N E T
A R E P O
S A T O R
```

Seven examples of the above inscription have been found, including two in Pompeii which were sealed in volcanic ash by the eruption of Mount Vesuvius in AD 79.

The reconstruction which is generally accepted indicates that the inscription is Christian. The letters in the square can be redistributed, with none spare, to make two As, two Os, and the words PATERNOSTER (Latin: Our Father) in both arms of a cross.

```
              A
              P
              A
              T
              E
              R
A PATERNOSTER O
              O
              S
              T
              E
              R
              O
```

A and O stand for the Greek letters alpha and omega, symbols for God in Revelation 1:8, 21:6 and 22:13. If this is a correct understanding it means that there were Christians in Pompeii by the seventies. This should cause no surprise, given the large Christian community in nearby Rome in the sixties, as attested by Tacitus.[2]

Tacitus: writing about the fire in Rome in AD 64

Tacitus (AD 55-c.120) was made governor of the province of Asia soon after Pliny's appointment to Bithynia, and something of his reputation as an historian may be discerned in part of the letter written to him by his friend Pliny:

> Thank you for asking me to send you a description of my uncle's death so that you can leave an accurate account of it for posterity... I know that immortal fame awaits him if his death is recorded by you...[3]

In his *Annals of Imperial Rome* written at about the same time as Pliny wrote the above letter, Tacitus describes how the Emperor Nero attempted to divert the blame for lighting the fire which destroyed three quarters of Rome, away from himself to a new and detested religious sect.

> But all human efforts, all the lavish gifts of the emperor, and the propitiations of the gods, did not banish the sinister belief that the conflagration was the result of an order. Consequently, to get rid of the report, Nero fastened the guilt and inflicted the most exquisite tortures on a class hated for their abominations, called Christians by the populace. Christus, from whom the name had its origin, suffered the extreme penalty during the reign of Tiberius at the hands of one of our procurators, Pontius Pilate, and a deadly superstition, thus checked for the moment, again broke out not only in Judaea, the first source of the evil, but also in the City [Rome], where all things hideous and shameful from every part of the world meet and become popular. Accordingly, an arrest was first made of all who confessed; then, upon their

information, an immense multitude was convicted, not so much of the crime of arson, as of hatred of the human race.[4]

It appears that Tacitus, like Pliny, despised but perhaps also feared this new movement. He describes the Christians as "a class hated for their abominations...a deadly superstition...evil...hideous...shameful". He accuses them of "hatred of the human race" which may refer to the Christian refusal to acknowledge Caesar as a god and the Roman state as divine.

In one sentence of the above passage Tacitus confirms five details mentioned in the New Testament:

1 The public career of Christ occurred in the time of the Emperor Tiberius (Luke 3:1).
2 Pontius Pilate was the Roman governor when Christ died. (Matthew 27:2; parallels in the other gospels; Acts 3:13 and 13:28).
3 Christ was executed as a criminal (Luke 23:2).
4 This occurred in Judaea (Mark 11:16).
5 The movement spread from Jerusalem to Rome (Acts 1:4 and 28:14).

This sentence agrees, in a broad sense, with the geographic sweep of Luke–Acts, a two-volume work which begins with Jesus in Judaea (Luke 2:4) and ends with Paul in Rome (Acts 28:14). Both the existence of Christ and the spread of early Christianity is confirmed by Tacitus.

This raises the question of why authors such as Pliny and Tacitus fail to say more about Jesus himself. In attempting an answer, we must stand in the shoes of these men. It is well to remember that both were from the upper strata of Roman society, and therefore very conservative. Aristocratic Romans were backward looking; they venerated Rome's illustrious past history, culture and institutions. They disliked change, specially when it came from non-Roman quarters such as Judaea. This is why Pliny and Tacitus both despised and feared the virulent new movement. It was a foreign superstition which was rapidly spreading like a disease across the empire. But perhaps Tacitus' reference to Christians in Rome as an "immense multitude" on one hand, or Pliny's of Christians in Bithynia as "a multitude of men" on the other, are exaggerations—propaganda to scare people? Here the evidence from the New Testament provides confirmation of the astonishing spread of the new movement. In AD 50 Paul's opponents in Macedonia complain that "These men...have turned the world upside down" (Acts 17:6), while in AD 62 the Jews in Rome ask the apostle about "this sect...that everywhere ...is spoken against" (Acts 28:22). The fears of Pliny and Tacitus were well grounded. Less than a century from the time they wrote, the Christian apologist Tertullian could claim:

> We are but of yesterday, and we have filled everything you have—cities, tenements, forts, towns...even the camps, tribes, palace, senate, forum. All we have left to you are the temples.[5]

What Pliny and Tacitus described was a movement several decades old, but which was by then worldwide and spreading rapidly. Inevitably it came to the attention of the writers of that time, though it is worth noticing that only part of the literature of the period has survived. But if a threatening movement was noticed by the Roman writers, a man on his own was not, especially if that man was a *crucified* Jew. Cicero, the Roman lawyer who lived before Christ, wrote:

> Even the mere word, *cross*, must remain far not only from the lips of the citizens of Rome, but also from their thoughts, their eyes, their ears... (*Pro Rabirio*: 5.16).

The reason Roman historians remain relatively silent about Jesus himself may be that crucifixion was unmentionable. Perhaps this is why Tacitus in another work, when reviewing the history of Judaea at the time of Jesus, said "under Tiberius all was quiet" (*History* 5:9, *sub Tiberio quies*).

Suetonius: writing about Rome c.AD 49

Suetonius (AD 69–c.140), in common with the other Roman writers, writes damningly of the Christians. He speaks of them as "... a class of man given to a new and wicked superstition".

"Class" suggests a group which was numerically significant while "new and wicked superstitition" conveys the revulsion many educated Romans felt towards the Christians.

In what is probably a reference to Christ, Suetonius relates an incident in the year AD 49 that, "Since the Jews constantly made disturbances at the instigation of Chrestus, he [Claudius] expelled them from Rome".[7]

If by "Chrestus" Suetonius is referring to Jesus "Christus", as most scholars believe, it means that there were Christians in Rome by AD 49. But this is only to corroborate what the Christian sources tell us.

When Paul arrived in Italy about AD 60, he met Christians at Puteoli in the south (Acts 28:14) and was welcomed by an advance party even before he reached Rome (Acts 28:15). About three years earlier, he had written his magnum opus, the *Letter to the Romans*, which virtually demanded the existence of a Christian community of some size to warrant the effort. He told them that their "faith is proclaimed in the whole world" (Romans 1:8) and that he had often "intended to come" to them (1:13, 15:22–24). Clearly the presence of Christians in Rome predates the letter by some years. In AD 49 the Emperor Claudius expelled the Jews from Rome because of problems caused by Christianity. Among them were Aquila and Priscilla who settled in Corinth and who were almost certainly Christians, (see Acts 18:2,3). If Aquila and Priscilla were in fact Christians, it is quite possible that they were involved in the disturbances about "Chrestus" which led to the mass expulsion of the Jews from Rome.

If there were Christians in Italy by the late forties, how did they come to be there? One thing that can be said is that, despite later church tradition, the movement was not brought initially by Peter or Paul. Peter was still in Palestine in the late forties (Galatians 2:11) and Paul did not arrive in Rome until the early sixties (Acts 28:14). While the two apostles may have helped to stabilise an already existent Christian community, its origin is probably due to the migration of Christian Jews from Judaea in the thirties and forties.

How large a movement was early Christianity? What do these Roman writers tell us?

The non-Christian sources, supported and supplemented by Christian sources, indicate the presence of Christians in Bithynia within the period c.64–110 and in Rome c.49–64. What is striking is the *number* of Christians involved. Pliny wrote of "many of all ages and every rank...from...not the cities only, but also villages and the country" whose presence had destroyed the ancient religions in Bithynia. This is a major movement. In writing of Claudius expelling all the Jews from Rome in AD 49 "at the instigation of Chrestus" we may take it that Suetonius is implying that the disturbances were of a most serious kind if they warranted the expulsion of many Jews from the City. Fifteen years later (AD 64), when the fire destroyed three quarters of the world capital and a suitable scapegoat was sought and found in the "class... called Christians" the implication again is that they must have been of a significant number. There would be no point in blaming a small or unknown group.

Although we cannot explain precisely how Christianity came to Bithynia or Rome, we can say that it originated with Jesus in Judaea. Who he was and what he did in Judaea, the epicentre, went unrecorded by Roman writers of the time. Nevertheless extensive shock waves rolled to the farthest shores of the Mediterranean world which in time left their marks in the records. The writers may have failed to take account of Jesus, the cause of it all, but they could hardly ignore the effects.

Benediction Twelve

After the disastrous war with the Romans AD 66–70, the Jewish Sanhedrin or Senate, ceased to exist as a political and administrative body. The Emperor Vespasian brought Judaea under direct military rule, leaving the Sanhedrin with a purely religious role. Most of the sects and parties within Judaism perished with the war. Two which survived were the Pharisees, representing the mainstream of Jewish religious life, and the Nazarenes, or Christians, who were by then regarded as heretical. In the eighties the Pharisee-dominated Sanhedrin meeting at Jamnia, a town to the east of Jerusalem, formulated the following synagogue prayer:

> For the renegades let there be no hope, and may the arrogant kingdom soon be rooted out in our days, and the Nazarenes and the minim perish as in a moment and be blotted out from the book of life and with the righteous may they not be inscribed. Blessed art thou, O Lord, who humblest the arrogant.[8]

References in the Talmud indicate that the "minim" and the "Nazarenes" usually refer to Christians. This bitter prayer clearly attests the existence of Christians in Judaea in the post-70 period and it represents a tragic contrast with the frequently happy relations of Christian Jews with their fellow Jews in the period before the war. From Christian sources we read of Jewish Christian priests (Acts 6:7) and Christian Pharisees (Acts 15:5) and of "many thousands...among the Jews...who have believed...all zealous for the law" (Acts 21:20). Opposition there may have been from Sadducean high priests (Acts 4:1–3) and Herod Agrippa (Acts 12:1–3) but the Pharisees appear either to have been neutral, as Rabbi Gamaliel was (Acts 5:34–39), or well-disposed like those who protested at the unjust death of James brother of Jesus (Josephus, *Antiquities* 20:197–203). The grim sentiments of *Benediction 12* reflect the thorough separation of synagogue and church after the end of the war in AD 70.

Rabbi Eliezer

Rabbi Eliezer, who is thought to have written the following comment in the nineties, reflects the same bitter attitude as that of the Pharisees towards the Christians in the post-70 period.

> Rabbi Eliezer said, Balaam looked forth and saw that there was a man, born of a woman, who should rise up and seek to make himself God, and to cause the whole world to go astray. Therefore God gave power to the voice of Balaam that all the peoples of the world might hear, and thus he spake, Give heed that ye go not astray after that man; for it is written, God is not man that he should lie. And if he says that he is God he is a liar, and he will deceive and say that he departeth and cometh again at the end. He saith and he shall not perform.[9]

Although Rabbi Eliezer does not name Jesus, the references to "born of a woman" and "departeth and cometh again at the end" show clearly that Jesus is in mind. The Rabbi is preaching a little sermon against Jesus based on Numbers 23:19 in which the prophet Balaam stated "God is not a man that he should lie". What Balaam foresaw, said the Rabbi, was "a man... who should...make himself God". God was warning "all the peoples of the world" through the words of Balaam, "that ye go not astray after that man". The claim that the early Christians believed Jesus was God and that he would come back again, is confirmed by these words of Rabbi Eliezer. By his words "cause the whole world to go astray", the Rabbi is stating that the movement created by this person was worldwide. References to Christians in Bithynia, Rome and Pompeii also confirm this.

Josephus

Josephus, an aristocratic Pharisee, was born in AD 37. During the war with the Romans AD 66–70 he was captured by the Romans, and later was paid a pension by successive Emperors for services rendered to the Imperial Family. Early in the nineties he wrote the *Jewish Antiquities*.

Pharisees were not always bitterly opposed to Christians, as the Jewish historian clearly shows. Before the war, in an interregnum between Roman governors (AD 62) the high priest Annas (son of Annas of the gospels)

> ...convened the judges of the Sanhedrin and brought before them a man named James, the brother of Jesus who was called the Christ, and certain others. He accused them of having transgressed the law and delivered them up to be stoned. Those of the inhabitants of the city who were considered the most fair-minded and who were strict in observance of the law were offended at this.[10]

Those who were "strict in observance of the law" must refer to Pharisees, which suggests that they showed a degree of sympathy to James, brother of Jesus, who was leader of the multitudinous Jerusalem church. The members of that church, Paul had been informed, were "all zealous for the law" (Acts 21:20), which explains why the Pharisees were favourably disposed towards James. James's reference to "many thousands" of such Jerusalem believers (Acts 21:20), whilst possibly an exaggeration, nevertheless confirms the impression given elsewhere of large numbers of people involved in Christianity, and that it was a worldwide movement.

In this extract, the authenticity of which is not in doubt, Josephus confirms two important pieces of information from the New Testament.

1 Jesus was "called Christ" (cf. Acts 2:36)
2 James was his brother (cf. Galatians 1:19)

Josephus indicates no doubt as to the genuine existence in history of either Jesus or James.

Disputed cases

Josephus refers to Jesus earlier in his *Antiquities* in a passage which is known to scholars as the *Testimonium Flavianum*:

About that time there lived Jesus, a wise man, if indeed one ought to call him a man. For he was one who wrought surprising feats and was a teacher of such people as accept the truth gladly. He won over many Jews and many of the Greeks. He was the Messiah. When Pilate, upon hearing him accused by men of the highest standing among us, had condemned him to be crucified, those who had in the first place come to love him did not give up their affection for him. On the third day he appeared to them restored to life, for the prophets of God had prophesied these and countless other marvellous things about him. And the tribe of the Christians so called after him, has still to this day not disappeared.[11]

While this passage is in all the extant manuscripts of the *Antiquities* and is externally attested by Church historian Eusebius, who quoted it exactly and in full in AD 325, there are many who question its authenticity. The major problem is that another Christian writer, Origen, writing a century earlier than Eusebius, remarked in passing that Josephus "did not believe in Jesus as the Christ",[12] which apparently contradicts the text as it stands. It may be that some zealous but misguided Christian has tampered with the text removing the words "so-called" before Christ, as in the passage referring to the death of James. If the text is amended along those lines it would make good sense of Origen's comment. Another problem is the expression "if it is possible to call him a man". Is this another Christian interpolation, reflecting the orthodox doctrine of the deity of Christ or was it a piece of mild sarcasm by Josephus knowing that deity claims were made for Jesus?

Those two problems apart, many scholars are prepared to accept much or all of the remainder of the text as genuine. I am impressed by the reference to the Christians as not being extinct "to this day" which echoes the same laissez-faire neutrality towards Christianity as shown by Josephus' fellow Pharisee Gamaliel back in the thirties (Acts 5:38–39). Also, I detect in Josephus' words, "wrought surprising feats...a teacher ..." an echo of yet another Pharisee, Nicodemus, who said that Jesus was a "teacher" who performed "signs" (John 3:2). Josephus refers to Jesus as "teacher" and miracle worker which supports from the comments on Nicodemus.

Finally the phrase "a wise man" is a favourable variation of "a charlatan man", a phrase used repeatedly for the turbulent would-be miracle working prophets whom Josephus vilifies elsewhere in his writings. Since Jesus was a non-violent, non-political miracle worker and teacher, he might well be referred to by Josephus as "a wise man". Rather than reject this extract altogether, it seems preferable to accept it with some deletions. In broad terms it confirms and amplifies the comments of Tacitus.

Other uncertain pieces of evidence are the human bone receptacles dated pre-50 which have written on them what may be two prayers to Jesus for the deceased people. One says "Jesus, save"; the other "Jesus, let him arise". These were discovered in Jerusalem by the Jewish scholar Professor Sukenik who believed they represented the earliest archaeological evidence for Christianity. However, the lettering is not clear and Sukenik's claim has been challenged.

A third uncertain case is the recently discovered letter written by the Jewish revolutionary leader, ben Kosiba. The writer speaks menacingly of "the Galileans", which is believed by many to mean "the Christians". Here is the letter in full:

> From Shimeon ben Kosiba to Yeshua ben Galoula and to the men of the fort, peace. I take heaven to witness against me that unless you mobilize [destroy?] the Galileans who are with you, every man, I will put fetters on your feet as I did to ben Aphlul.[13]

Yigael Yadin, who discovered the letter in a cave near the Dead Sea, rejects the suggestion that "Galileans" means Christians. Ben Kosiba, however, is known from other sources to have persecuted Christians. The Christian writer Justin Martyr, a contemporary of ben Kosiba, commented that:

> In the present Jewish war it was only Christians whom bar Chocheba [another name for Kosiba], the leader of the rebellion of the Jews, commanded to be punished severely if they did not deny Jesus as the messiah of the Jews and blaspheme him.[14]

These were Christian Jews who, in their loyalty to Jesus, apparently refused to recognise ben Kosiba as Messiah. They may also have declined to take part in the uprising, following the example of the Jerusalem Church which withdrew from the war zone during the first Jewish war AD 66–70. Thus ben Kosiba had two reasons to punish the Christians: they did not recognise him, and they refused to fight in his war. Ben Kosiba's reference to "Galileans" may well refer to Christians.

SUMMARY OF THE NON-CHRISTIAN EVIDENCE

On the basis of this evidence from non-Christian sources, it is possible to draw the following conclusions:

1 Jesus Christ was executed (by crucifixion?) in Judaea during the period when Tiberius was Emperor (AD 14–37) and Pontius Pilate was Governor (AD 26–36).   Tacitus

2 The movement spread from Judea to Rome.	Tacitus
3 Jesus claimed to be God and that he would depart and return.	Eliezer
4 His followers worshipped him as (a) god.	Pliny
5 He was called "the Christ".	Josephus
6 His followers were called "Christians".	Tacitus, Pliny
7 They were numerous in Bithynia and Rome.	Tacitus, Pliny
8 It was a world-wide movement.	Eliezer
9 His brother was James.	Josephus

While this evidence is not extensive, it is noteworthy that it does not in any way conflict with, but rather confirms, the historical information in the New Testament.

Further reading to Chapter Two:

F.F. Bruce, *Jesus and Christian Origins outside the New Testament*, Eerdmans, Grand Rapids, 1974.

R. Dunkerley, *Beyond the Gospels*, Pelican, Harmondsworth, 1957.

H.C. Kee, *Jesus in History*, Harcourt, Brace & World, Inc., 1970.

J. Klausner, *Jesus of Nazareth*, George Allen & Unwin, London, 1925.

Notes

[1]*Epistles* 10:96 quoted in J. Stevenson, *A New Eusebius*, S.P.C.K., London, 1960, p.14.

[2]*See* further, J. Stevenson (ed.), *A New Eusebius*, S.P.C.K., London, 1960, (pp.7–8).

[3]*Epistles*, 6:16.

32

[4]*Annals*, 15:44, 2-5.

[5]*Apology*, 37:4.

[6]*Life of Nero* 16:2.

[7]*Life of Claudius*, 25:4 cf. Acts 18:2.

[8]*Benediction 12*, quoted in C.K. Barrett, *The New Testament Background*, S.P.C.K., London, 1961, p.167.

[9]J. Klausner, *Jesus of Nazareth*, Collier-Macmillan, London, 1929, (p.34).

[10]*Antiquities*, 20:197-203.

[11]*Antiquities*, 18:63,64.

[12]*Contra Celsum*, 1:47.

[13]Y. Yadin, *Bar-Kokhba*, London, 1978, (p.137).

[14]Quoted in Eusebius, *Ecclesiastical History*, 4:8, (Loeb Classical Library), Heinemann, 1926.

CHAPTER THREE

Fixing the Time-Frame

Useful as the non-biblical information is in establishing that Jesus really lived, the evidence of the New Testament is both earlier and more extensive.

"But," you say, "I cannot be expected to believe that. The New Testament was all written by Christians". This is an understandable reaction and I can sympathize with it. But let me make two comments.

First, the holding of personal convictions doesn't necessarily mean blindness or dishonesty. A biographer may admire a statesman so much that he goes to the trouble to research and write about him. If he the writer is competent and well-balanced he will not omit the shortcomings and failures of his subject. Admiration may be the motive in writing, but it does not of itself destroy objectivity; this depends on the integrity of the writer. Luke admired Paul and was his friend, yet he does not conceal Paul's unChristlike reaction when struck at the command of the high priest (Acts 23:3). Mark was a convinced follower of Jesus, and yet he doesn't omit the cursing of the fig tree (Mark 11:12–14), an incident which has troubled many people. Similarly John, the beloved disciple, records Jesus speaking to his mother in what appears to be a harsh way (John 2:4). In fact, the presence in the new Testament of details which we find awkward, points to realism and honesty in the apostolic writers.

Second, the New Testament did not always exist as a single volume. Some people believe that the apostles called a meeting and decided who would write which part—"Matthew, Mark, Luke, John, you each write a gospel and Paul, you write some letters. And let us put it all together in one book". Let me say, quite definitely, that the books of the New Testament were not written and collected like that.

Paul wrote to the Galatians because they were getting away from the gospel message. The Corinthians had some practical problems which they listed in a letter; First Corinthians is Paul's answer to these and other matters. Mark was written to set down information about Jesus in a more permanent form and also to bring the good news about Jesus to a particular group of readers, probably Greek-speaking Romans. The books of the New Testament were not written by people hermetically sealed off from life—quite the opposite, in fact. Every part of the New Testament is, as far as I can see, a response to real life needs. It is a collection of "occasional" literature, each part written for some specific occasion or purpose.

Moreover, the New Testament writers were not in league with each other at the point of writing. Nothing Mark wrote indicates any verbal influence by Paul, or vice versa. John did not depend on Paul nor, many scholars believe, upon Mark. While Luke and Matthew have used Mark, their gospels appear to have been written independently of each other and of John. While James, Hebrews and First Peter hold some ideas in common with Paul, none of them appears to have been influenced by, or to be dependent upon, any other. This literary independence reflects the fact that the writers were active missionaries whose spheres of work were both specialized in themselves and also, to a significant degree, remote from one another.

Further, it is quite certain that the literature was not

collected into a single entity quickly, but over a consider-able period of time. Paul wrote to the Colossians and the Laodiceans (whose letter has been lost) requesting that the letters be exchanged and read in both churches (Colossians 4:16). We may assume that the churches copied the originals for re-reading and also exchanged letters with one another. But it took many years before the books of the New Testament were widely circulated and collected.

The New Testament existed in the first place as many separate parts, written separately and circulated separately. The parts were only finally recognised as belonging to one official volume or "canon" in the fourth century, though the principle of recognition existed from the earliest times. Because the parts were produced separately and independently, we have a number of built-in means of checking one against the other. Since there are seven or eight independently written accounts which refer to Jesus, it is as reasonable to believe he existed as it is to believe a road accident happened because seven or eight people independently said it did. The evidence for Christ is to be accepted or rejected in much the same way a judge and jury accept or reject evidence from witnesses to an accident or a crime.

Fixing the time-frame of Paul's letters

The time-frame of the missionary career of Paul can be fixed with almost complete certainty. When Paul arrived in Corinth, he met Aquila and Priscilla who had recently "come from Italy...because Claudius had commanded all the Jews to leave Rome" (Acts 18:2). This dovetails with the Roman historian Suetonius who wrote that Claudius banished from Rome all Jews because they were continually making disturbances about Christ and Christianity.[1] Scholars of Roman history date this expulsion to c.AD 49. We conclude that Paul arrived in Corinth some time during AD 50. This is confirmed by an inscription which fixes the beginning of Gallio's one year appointment as proconsul in Achaia at July 51, a detail that corresponds with the reference in Acts that "while Gallio was proconsul of Achaia, the Jews made a united attack on Paul and brought him into court" (Acts 18:12). Since First Thessalonians was, by common consent, written from Corinth soon after Paul's arrival there (1 Thessalonians 3:6, and Acts 18:5), we conclude that this letter was written in AD 50. This represents the earliest generally accepted extremity of the time-frame. Few scholars dispute this date, although some may place Paul's letter to the Galatians earlier, about AD 48.

The other extremity of the time-frame is fixed by the decision of Festus, Roman Procurator of Judaea, to despatch Paul to Rome (Acts 25:12). Historians set the date for the arrival of Festus in Judaea at about AD 60. The author of Acts, who was with Paul, is quite specific. No more than two weeks after his arrival, Festus convened the hearing in which he decided to send Paul to be tried by Caesar (Acts 25:1-6). Paul's departure for Rome must have followed shortly after that (Acts 25:13,23; 27:1). We conclude that Paul set out for Rome in AD 60 and arrived after many adventures some time early the next year (Acts 27:9 and 27; 28:11-17). Acts concludes with a reference to Paul's two-year imprisonment in Rome, that is in AD 61 and 62, during which time he probably wrote the letter to the Philippians (Philippians 1:7,13; 4:22).

The fourth century Christian writer Eusebius states that Paul was executed in Rome under Nero.[2] Since Nero died in AD 68, Paul's death obviously occurred sometime between AD 63 and AD 68 thereby setting the latter extremity of his letter writing.

Thus the time-frame for Paul's letters is from about AD 50 to the middle-late sixties. Why am I making so much of the time-frame for Paul's writings? It is because, on the one hand it can be established with such complete confidence, and on the other, because it is so close in time to the life and death of Jesus of Nazareth. According to Tacitus, Jesus was executed in Judaea in the time of Pontius Pilate who was governor AD 26–36. Evidence from the gospels and from calendar calculations has fixed the date of the crucifixion as either AD 30 or 33.

If Jesus died in AD 33, as many believe, then a mere seventeen years separates that event from the earliest (?) of Paul's letters, First Thessalonians. In that letter Paul writes that "the Jews...killed the Lord Jesus" (1 Thessalonians 2:15). Based on the early evidence from Paul, there can be no reasonable doubt that Jesus was a genuine figure of history.

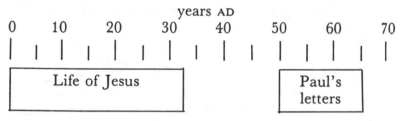

Fixing the time-frame for the rest of the New Testament

If we can "fix" Paul's writings to a particular period, what about the other fourteen parts of the New Testament, in particular the gospels? Here we have a problem. We are able to establish a time-frame for Paul because of the Acts of the Apostles and also because of such external milestones as Gallio's appointment in Achaia, the expulsion of the Jews from Rome and the arrival of Festus in Judaea. But there is no documentary evidence external to the gospels which states when they were written, and the writers themselves do not say. The same is true of the remaining ten pieces of the New Testament.

In the absence of external documentary evidence, some scholars appeal to the evidence of events such as Nero's persecutions of Christians in Rome beginning in AD 64 and the devastating war in Palestine AD 66–70 which culminated in the demolition of the temple in

Jerusalem. These events were so momentous that, it is argued, they must have some echo within the New Testament. Thus it is suggested that First Peter must be dated shortly before AD 64 because of the references to impending persecution (1 Peter 1:6,7; 3:13-17; 4:12-19; 5:8-11). The references in the letter to the Hebrews to high priests and sacrifices (Hebrews 5:1-4; 10:11) have been taken to suggest that the Temple was still in use and that the letter must accordingly be earlier than AD 70. With respect to the non-Pauline part of the New Testament, J.A.T. Robinson has argued that the lack of any reference to the Jewish–Roman war AD 66-70 may mean that every part of the New Testament was written beforehand.[3]

All that can be said in these matters, however, is that a case can be made but not proved. The problem is that the evidence is circumstantial and sometimes ambiguous. At this stage in New Testament study there is no consensus about the precise dating of the non-Pauline literature. In the absence of new evidence, New Testament scholars will continue to express different opinions about the dates.

Although no one can say exactly when the gospels were written, we can say with certainty by which dates they were in circulation. There is external documentary evidence by which we can fix the outer limits of the time-frame.

The coming of Jesus and the activity of the apostles, spoken and written, sparked off an explosion of Christian literature in the second and third centuries. Three authors wrote close to the year 100—Clement in about 96, Ignatius in about 108 and Polycarp in about 110. What is significant for this discussion is that these writers quote from, or refer to, many books of the New Testament.

In the first dozen sentences of Polycarp's letter to the Philippians, written in about 110, he quotes from Acts, First Peter, Ephesians and the gospel of Matthew, thus establishing that these books were in use by the time he wrote. Altogether Polycarp[4] attests the existence of:

Matthew	Acts	Romans	Hebrews
Mark		1 Corinthians	1 Peter
Luke		2 Corinthians	1 John
John		Galatians	
		Ephesians	
		Philippians	
		Colossians	
		2 Thessalonians	
		1 Timothy	
		2 Timothy	

18 by 110

In his seven short letters written, c.108, Ignatius[5] quotes or refers to:

Matthew	Acts	Romans	Hebrews
Mark		1 Corinthians	James
Luke		2 Corinthians	1 Peter
John		Galatians	2 Peter
		Ephesians	1 John
		Philippians	3 John
		Colossians	Revelation
		1 Thessalonians	
		1 Timothy	
		2 Timothy	
		Titus	
		Philemon	

24 by 108

Clement,[6] writing from Rome to Corinth, c.96, refers to:

Matthew	Romans	Hebrews
Mark	1 Corinthians	James
Luke	Ephesians	1 Peter
	1 Timothy	
	Titus	

11 by 96

On the basis of these three early Christian authors it can be stated that twenty-five pieces of the New Testament were definitely in circulation by about the year 100.

25 NT books by 100

By that date First Thessalonians had been in use for fifty years. The non-Pauline pieces quoted or referred to may have been in use for a comparable period, but unfortunately there is no way of knowing for certain. The point I am making is that attestation by Clement in c.96 of, let us say, Mark does not imply that Mark was necessarily of recent composition. It could just as easily have been in circulation for three or four decades. The silence of Clement, Ignatius and Polycarp with respect to 2 John and Jude need not imply that these books were not written, only that those authors failed to quote from them or refer to them.

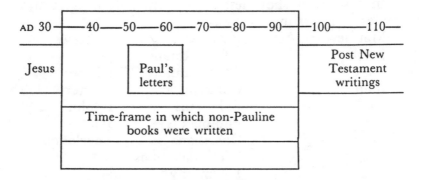

To summarise the evidence relating to the time-frame, two statements can be made with confidence:

1 Paul's letters were written in the period c.50–c.65.

2 Apart from 2 John and Jude for which there are no sure references, the remaining parts of the New Testament were written after c.33 and were in use by the nineties.

It is instructive to compare the literary evidence for Jesus with that of other famous men of antiquity. Roughly comparable is Tiberius, the emperor in whose time Jesus died. Born 42 BC, Tiberius was emperor AD 14–37. While

Velleius Paterculus wrote in about AD 30 of Tiberius' earlier military exploits, our major sources are considerably later—Tacitus about AD 110, Suetonius about AD 120, Dio Cassius about AD 220.

In Jesus' case there is a shorter time lapse between his life and the literature. Allowing c.90 as the latest date possible for the gospels, less than sixty years separate these books from their principal character. At the end of the frame nearer Jesus we note that a mere seventeen years elapsed between Jesus and First Thessalonians.

A more extreme comparison might be made between Alexander the Great, who died 323 BC and his major historian, Arrian, who wrote AD 130s. The major outlines of Alexander's career are not doubted despite a period exceeding four hundred years separating the man and the chief source of information about him.

It is important to note three things about Jesus in the context of history-writing in the ancient world.

First, the time lapse between his life and the literature about it is short compared to that between the lives and the literature about other great figures of the times.

Second, the number of authors contributing to the literature also compares very favourably with the number writing about other great figures. No less than nine or ten early authors, most of them writing independently of each other, refer to Jesus.

Third, from the end of the epoch of the New Testament writings there was an unbroken and growing stream of Christian literature which establishes the existence of the literature of the New Testament by quoting from it. To this point we now turn.

Further reading to Chapter Three:
F.F. Bruce, *The New Testament Documents*, I.V.P., Leicester, 1979.

42

J.A.T. Robinson, *Re-dating the New Testament*, S.C.M.
London, 1976.

Notes
[1]*Claudius*, 25.

[2]*Historia Ecclesia*, II 25:28.

[3]J.A.T. Robinson, *Redating the New Testament*, S.C.M. Press,
London, 1976.

[4]J.B. Lightfoot, *The Apostolic Fathers*, Part Two, Volume III, 1885,
"Index of Scriptural Passages", pp.522, 523.

[5]*Op. cit.*, pp.520–522.

[6]A. Roberts and J. Donaldson (eds), *The Ante-Nicene Fathers*, Vol I,
W.B. Eerdmans, Grand Rapids, Footnotes, pp.5–21.

CHAPTER FOUR

Is the Transmission Trustworthy?

The next logical question is: how do I know that what I now read in the New Testament is what was originally written? After all, nineteen hundred years have passed and the text could easily have been tampered with during that period. How trustworthy is the transmission?

An unusual habit
"It was their habit on a fixed day to assemble," wrote Pliny, governor of Bithynia, informing Emperor Trajan about the meetings of the sect of the Christians. The assembling of Christians on a "fixed day" is taken for granted today. In the year AD 112 it was an oddity, something worth noting. At first they met in homes or in the open and only after several centuries in special Christian buildings. But wherever it was, meet they did—and on "a fixed day".

Forty or so years later, the Christian writer Justin described what happened in Rome when Christians assembled for their weekly meeting. This short extract shows how important the reading of the scriptures was:

On the day called Sunday all who live in cities or in the country gather together to the one place, and the memoirs of the apostles or the writings of the prophets are read, as long as time permits.[1]

In Justin's day in Rome the "memoirs of the apostles", as he calls the gospels, had been copied from earlier versions which went back less than a century to the Greek originals written by Matthew, Mark, Luke and John. We have no way of knowing how much hand copying stood between the "memoirs" mentioned by Justin and the originals, but it cannot have been many, given the slowness and expense of the copying process and the relatively brief space of time.[2]

Half a century after Justin, these Greek documents were translated into Latin for reading in Latinized North Africa, Gaul, and Spain as well as Italy. The gospel spread quickly throughout the polyglot societies surrounding the Mediterranean. By the third and fourth centuries the New Testament was being translated into Coptic and Syriac. And so the process went on. In every country the gospel went to, in time local translations were made for the public reading of the scriptures to the Christians assembled on a "fixed day" of the week.

This unusual "habit" of weekly meeting, which struck Pliny as worth noticing, continued uninterrupted through the centuries and has remained a mark of Christianity. Sunday-by-Sunday, the public reading of the scriptures has occurred from apostolic times until today.

Profusion of manuscripts

The "habit" of meeting accompanied as it was by public scripture reading led to the proliferation and therefore the preservation of the scriptures. In the early centuries the rapidly growing number of churches required an increased supply of copies. There still exist more than five thousand early manuscript copies of part or whole of the New Testament in Greek. In addition, there are numerous early translations into Coptic, Latin, Syriac, Armenian, Georgian, etc. These are called the "Versions". Let us not forget that Christianity spread in an unorganised, unco-ordinated way. There can be no question of centralized publishing of these manuscripts.

So the expansion of the movement was matched by a profusion of manuscripts many of which have survived through to modern times. For example, Codex Sinaiticus, a complete fourth century edition of the New Testament today is safely housed in the British Museum. Codex Sinaiticus was discovered in 1844 by Count Tischendorf at St Catherine's monastery, Mt Sinai. Codex Sinaiticus owes its survival, like many other New Testament manuscripts, to a dry climate and the relative security of a Christian monastery.

This profusion of early manuscripts of the New Testament is in contrast with the few for Josephus' *Jewish War*. Josephus, a Pharisee and Jewish aristocrat, wrote his great history of the war of AD 66–70 between the Romans and Jews shortly after its cessation. It is a Greek work based on an Aramaic first draft, and written very close in time to the gospels. Apart from two collections of excerpts, there are only nine complete manuscripts in existence, the oldest of which is a fifth century Latin translation. The remaining eight Greek manuscripts, of which only two are regarded as superior texts, are from the tenth century and later. If scholars are confident, as they are, of the integrity of Josephus' restored text, though based on so few and such late manuscripts, how much more might we be assured about the restored text of the Greek New Testament, based as it is on so many and such early manuscripts?

The contrast is even more dramatic with Tacitus' *Annals of Imperial Rome*, the chief historical source for the Roman world of New Testament times. There is only one surviving manuscript for *Annals* 1 to 6 (discovered c.1510) and one for *Annals* 11 to 16 (discovered c.1430). Neither manuscript is earlier than the Middle Ages. *Annals* 7 to 10 is missing.

Clearly it was that Christian "habit" of assembling on

a "fixed day" to hear the scriptures read, which explains both the multiplicity and the survival of New Testament texts. During the Middle Ages these early manuscripts were kept secure by the monasteries. Today they are stored in modern libraries under carefully controlled conditions.

An avalanche of early Christian books

While Christianity had small beginnings in the first half century of its life, it rapidly expanded throughout the Graeco–Roman world in the subsequent centuries. Only two centuries after the last book of the New Testament, Revelation, was written, the Emperor Constantine virtually made Christianity the official religion of the Roman Empire. Throughout those two hundred years Christian intellectuals and leaders had been writing books defending and explaining the faith. Their collected writings comprise the ten large volumes of the *Ante-Nicene Library*, each volume being several times longer than the whole New Testament.

These writers often quoted at length from the New Testament and their quotations, called "citations", are used as a check on the early manuscripts of the New Testament. It has been claimed that almost the whole New Testament could be recovered from the citations of those early Christian writers. Their books, like the New Testament manuscripts, were preserved through the Middle Ages by the monasteries.

When Josephus and Tacitus completed their manuscripts there was no immediate system for either preserving or copying what they had written. With the New Testament it was different. That collection of books became the much-copied Scriptures of a rapidly growing movement which soon became the state religion. Those Scriptures in turn gave rise to an immense output of early Christian literature which quoted them at great length and, in effect, preserved them. The growth of the monasteries in the fourth century, coincided with the beginning of the Dark Ages. It was in the monasteries that the New Testament manuscripts, the writings of the early Church and the work of such writers as Josephus and Tacitus were preserved until the Renaissance, the invention of the printing press, and the development of modern museums and libraries.

How confident is the modern scholar that the Greek text of the New Testament which he translates is as originally written?

Through the labours of textual critics who have collected and compared the manuscripts over the past two centuries, it can be stated that the major questions about the text have been resolved. For example, Mark 16:9 to 20 and John 8:1 to 11 are now believed not to have belonged to the original text of those gospels. Apart from those two longer passages, what remain are numerous variant readings of individual words or short phrases. The footnotes of the Revised Standard Version of the Bible indicate the major variants, which occur at the rate of less than one per page. It is safe to say that substantial matters of Christian history or doctrine are not affected by whatever uncertainties remain. In reviewing the state of textual criticism Stephen Neill has commented that:

> We have a far better and more reliable text of the New Testament than of any other ancient work whatever, and the measure of uncertainty is really rather small.[3]

Neill concluded:

> Anyone who reads the New Testament in any one of half a dozen recent Greek editions, or in any modern translation, can feel confident that, though there may be uncertainties in detail, in almost everything of importance he is close indeed to the text of the New Testament books as they were originally written.[4]

Further reading to Chapter Four:
B. Metzger, *A Textual Commentary on the Greek New Testament*, United Bible Societies, London, 1971.
S. Neill, *The Interpretation of the New Testament 1861–1961*, O.U.P., London, 1964.
A. Souter, *The Text and Canon of the New Testament*, Duckworth, London, 1960.

Notes
[1]Justin, *First Apology*, 67.

[2]The time a trained scribe took to copy the four gospels has been estimated at six weeks, or about three months for the whole New Testament. *See* Wm. Barclay, *The Gospels and Acts*, S.C.M. London, 1976, Vol.1, p.25.

[3]Stephen Neill, *The Interpretation of the New Testament 1861–1961*, O.U.P., London, 1964, p.78.

[4]*Op. cit.*, p.81.

CHAPTER FIVE

The Two Witnesses

So far we have attempted to ask and answer the following questions: Did Jesus in fact live? Yes. The early non-Christian writers leave us in no doubt. Can we know the time-frame in which the New Testament was written? Again, yes. In broad terms the literature came into existence within the period AD 33 to 95. Can we be confident about transmission of the manuscripts from those times to the present? Once more, yes. The sheer numbers of early texts guarantee that what we read is, for all practical purposes, what the original authors wrote.

The next logical question is: can we know that what we read of Jesus is a true account? Perhaps the story has been twisted somewhere in the period between Jesus' life and the time the literature about him was written. How confident may we be that Matthew, Mark, Luke and John have told us the truth about Jesus and not given us some idealised, romantic version?

Scholars of the New Testament have wrestled with this question for two centuries and still much work remains to be done. There are three matters, however, which have been resolved to the satisfaction of most of the experts.

1 Mark was written before Matthew and Luke.
2 Matthew and Luke broadly follow Mark's sequence and incorporate Markan material into their gospels. Matthew, Mark and Luke are often called

"synoptic" gospels which means they are able to be arranged in parallel.[1]

3   John's outline of events does not easily dovetail with Mark's or vice versa.[2]

For the time being we will leave Matthew and Luke and concentrate on Mark and John, whose presentations of the career of Jesus are so different. In Mark's account Jesus comes to Jerusalem only once—for the final week of his earthly life. By contrast John often has Jesus in Jerusalem. In fact, sixteen of John's twenty-one chapters are set in Jerusalem. Clearly Mark and John are *un*synoptic.

What makes the gospels of Mark and John important is the concept of "witness". The writer of the fourth gospel makes direct claim to be a "witness" to Jesus (John 21:20,24 compare 19:35). In the other case there is early evidence that Mark wrote in collaboration with Peter, who often claims to be a "witness" to Jesus (Acts 2:32; 3:15; 5:32; 10:39–42; 1 Peter 5:1; 2 Peter 1:16–18). We defer for the moment for the discussion of the claims that the gospels of John and Mark arise out of "witness". First we must ask, what is "witness"?

Witness in the New Testament

Christians today sometimes speak about "witnessing", by which they mean sharing their faith in an evangelistic way. In this context "witness" means telling about something which is personal, religious and subjective. But this is not the way "witness" is used in the New Testament.

The noun "witness" is used thirty-five times in the New Testament. Leaving aside the five references in the Book of Revelation where it is used in the sense of "martyr", the remaining thirty are used in the sense of "*eye*witness". Here the dominant idea is of an onlooker who could "bear witness" in a court hearing for or against an accused person. The letter to the Hebrews comments that:

A man who has violated the law of Moses dies without mercy at the testimony of two or three *witnesses* (10:28).[3]

Any charge against an erring Christian (2 Corinthians 13:1; Matthew 18:16) or local church leader (1 Timothy 5:19) is, by the rule of the Old Testament (Deuteronomy 19:15), to be sustained by "two or three witnesses". At the trials of both Jesus (Mark 14:63) and Stephen (Acts 6:14, 7:58) evidence was given by "witnesses". These references indicate that a "witness" was someone who had been present at the time of an incident and who could give evidence of what he had seen or heard. It is the same idea when Paul calls "God to witness against" him (2 Corinthians 1:23; compare Romans 1:9; Philippians 1:8).

It is in this sense that the apostles were to be "witnesses" to Christ (Acts 1:8). The death of Judas left a gap to be filled to make up the number to twelve apostles (Acts 1:20). Peter stated the qualifications for the person to be chosen:

One of the men who have accompanied us during all the time that the Lord Jesus went in and out among us, beginning from the baptism of John until the day he was taken up from us—one of these men must become with us a *witness* to his resurrection (Acts 1:21-22).[5]

Notice here two qualifications about the would-be apostle and "witness": he must have belonged to the physical company of those who were present with Jesus from the beginning of his public ministry until his ascension; and he must be able, therefore, to "witness" to the resurrection of Jesus as one who had been present at the time.

As the narrative of Acts unfolds, Peter repeatedly claims to have been a "witness" to (the death) and resurrection of Jesus:

This Jesus God raised up, and of that we are all *witnesses.* (2:32)

...the author of life, whom God raised from the dead. To this we are *witnesses.* (3:15)

The God of our fathers raised Jesus... And we are *witnesses* to these things. (5:30,32)

God raised him on the third day and made him manifest; not to all the people but to us who were chosen by God as *witnesses*. (10:40–41)[3]

Acting as a "witness" meant telling others what you had actually seen or heard with as much exactness as if giving evidence in a trial. In these references "witness" did not relate primarily to inward religious experience. "Witness" is about hard facts, about details of date, time, place and circumstances of empirical and observable events.

The seriousness of false witness

Some of the Corinthians were doubting that there would be a resurrection of the dead (1 Corinthians 15:12), doubtless preferring the Greek idea of the immortality of the soul. In attempting to deal with this, Paul reminded them of the fundamentals of the apostolic gospel as received by him and handed over to them. The appropriate details to underline were that "Christ was raised on the third day" (1 Corinthians 15:4) and "that he appeared to Cephas...to the twelve...to more than five hundred brothers...to James...to all the apostles...last of all...also to me" (15:5–8). By his words "whether then it was I or they, so we preach and so you believed" (15:11), Paul means simply that "Jesus was seen by us risen from the dead; we told you about it and you believed".

Paul's logic is simple. If Christ has not been raised then what we have said about seeing him is empty and, what is worse, we who have spoken have misrepresented God because we have "witnessed" that God did something which he did not in fact do. Paul and his fellow apostles and fellow witnesses will have been guilty of the ultimate blasphemy in lying about an important action of God. It was one thing in a law court solemnly to give evidence as a "witness"; it was another to put God in the dock and to lie about his actions. In speaking as a "witness" to the resurrection of Jesus, nothing less than the truthfulness and integrity of God was at stake. It is as if Paul shudders at the implications.

The New Testament writers keep these things in clear focus. You either were a "witness" or you were not. If Peter knew he was a "witness. . . of Christ" he also knew that the readers of his first letters had not seen Christ (1 Peter 5:1 and 1:8). On the other hand, Luke knew that he was not an eyewitness, while others before him *were* eyewitnesses of Christ (Luke 1:2). Similarly, the anonymous writer to the Hebrews declares himself to have heard, not the Lord, but those who heard him (Hebrews 2:3). The disclaimers of Luke and the anonymous writer make the claims of Peter all the more impressive. Only if you had seen and heard the Lord were you qualified to be a "witness".

This then is the background to the full meaning of "witness" and the claims made by John and for Mark. It is important, however, that we take careful note of what they write and why. John calls his work "a book" written so that the reader may "believe that Jesus is the Christ, the Son of God" (John 20:30,31). This suggests that John may be writing for those who already have some knowledge of Jesus to ensure that what they believe about him is correct. To this end the author has selected and written about just a few of the miracle signs of Jesus. He specifically claims not to have written comprehensively (John 20:30).

In his opening sentence, Mark refers to his document as a "gospel" which means "an important announcement of good news", either written or spoken. To look no further than Mark 1:14—we read of Jesus *speaking* the gospel. Unlike John, Mark does not tell us exactly why he is writing. We have to look for clues. While one purpose may be to give instruction and encouragement to believers (Mark 13:37) another may be to confront the non-Christian so that he will, like the centurion, declare Jesus to be "the Son of God" (15:39).

Thus our two documents are called by different titles and appear to have somewhat different objectives as well as different audiences. Mark is certainly written for Gentiles (see the author's explanation of Jewish customs in 7:3,4 and 14:12). John appears to be written for Greek speaking Jews—note the relative absence of explanations of things Jewish.

Stylistically, these two works differ both from each other and from a modern biography. A biographer today would be expected to describe the parents of the chief character, the circumstances of his birth, as well as his education, appearance and upbringing—details which Mark and John do not supply. It is important to read these texts on their terms, not on ours. While an historian may gather many facts about Jesus from John and Mark, it is extremely unlikely that he will then be able to write a biography in the modern manner. Each author has a message—a message about Jesus—which he expects us to recognize and accept. Each gospel is biographical but not a biography, historical but not a history. Biographies supply comprehensive information to inform the mind of the reader; gospels inform the mind about Jesus in order to challenge the reader's will and behaviour. It has been said that they read you as you read them. The gospels address the whole person, not the intellect alone.

Did John and Mark know one another's writings? Scholars disagree about this but, it appears to me that our authors wrote independently of each other. Apart from their accounts of Good Friday and Easter Day, the only other narratives common to both are the baptism of John, the clearing of the temple, the feeding of the multitude, the anointing and the triumphal entry. The stories are told so differently that the possibility of literary dependence seems remote.

Further, how does one account for an innocent divergence such as the hour of the crucifixion? While both authors agree that the crucifixion occurred on the day before the Sabbath (John 19:31; Mark 15:42), in Mark Jesus is crucified at "the third hour" (9 a.m. see 15:25) while in John the trial before Pilate is still in progress at "the sixth hour" (12 noon see 19:14). While for some this difference is unpalatable, it may, in fact, enhance the deeper historicity of the account. Perfect agreement in every detail might justifiably arouse a suspicion of some kind of collusion between the authors. As they stand, the two versions, with their distinctive styles and various loose ends, encourage confidence that our writers are men of truth writing independently of each other, and that through them we, the readers, are in contact with the events as they occurred.

The Old Testament called for not one but "two or three witnesses" (Deuteronomy 19:15). In the gospels of John and Mark we have two independent, written "witnesses" to Jesus. Through their "witness" we, the readers, are able to arrive at a verdict, based on evidence, about Jesus of Nazareth.

Further reading to Chapter Five:

J.D. Douglas (ed.), *The Illustrated Bible Dictionary*, I.V.P., Leicester, 1980, articles on "John the Apostle" and "Peter".

L.L. Morris, *This is the Testimony*, Baker Memorial Lecture, Ridley College, Melbourne, 1970.

H.E.W. Turner, *Jesus, Master and Lord*, Mowbrays, London, 1957.

Notes
[1]"Having an approximately parallel point of view", *World Book Dictionary*, Chicago, 1968.

[2]And, therefore, with neither Matthew's nor Luke's Gospel.

[3]My italics.

CHAPTER SIX

Witness One: The Disciple Whom Jesus Loved

The author of the fourth gospel makes the direct claim to have been a witness of Jesus. In his account of the crucifixion, he describes how the soldiers broke the legs of the other victims before discovering that Jesus was already dead, whereupon a soldier "pierced his side with a spear". The writer then adds:

He who saw it has borne witness—his testimony is true, and he knows that he tells the truth—that you also may believe (John 19:35).

The context makes it clear that the only disciple near the scene of the crucifixion was "the disciple whom [Jesus] loved" (19:26). He saw what happened and bore witness about it. Further, he assures his readers that his testimony is true and may be believed.

The final episode in this gospel is a dialogue between Jesus and Peter, in which Peter enquires what is to happen to "the disciple whom Jesus loved" who was following them (21:20,21). The author continues:

This is the disciple who is bearing witness to these things, and who has written these things; and we know that his testimony is true (21:24).

This is *written* witness by the "disciple whom Jesus loved", who was present with Jesus and Peter by the Sea of Tiberias when for the third time since his crucifixion Jesus manifested himself alive to his disciples (21:14). The writer of this book intends us to understand that he is the "disciple whom Jesus loved".

Who, then, are those who are referred to as "we" and who know that the testimony of the beloved disciple is true? It is sometimes suggested that these persons are in fact responsible for writing the fourth gospel. The text, however, clearly states "this is the disciple...who has written these things", referring to the disciple whom Jesus loved. Those who are described as "we" authenticate what is written but they are not the authors. But who are they?

The clue to their identity is found at the beginning of John's book—"we have beheld his glory" (1:14). When he subsequently states "Jesus...manifested his glory and his disciples believed in him" (2:11), it is clear that, since "glory" is present in both passages, "his disciples" in chapter two are the "we" of chapter one. Clearly, then, the "we" represents the disciples who accompanied Jesus and who witnessed his signs. (*See* John 20:30).

This book, however, implies that the group continued and that it was only after Jesus left them that many of the things he said and did were understood. After the temple-clearing incident the author comments:

When...he was raised from the dead, his disciples *remembered* that he had said this; and they believed the Scripture and the word which Jesus had spoken (2:22).[1]

Similarly he observes, after the entry to Jerusalem, that:

His disciples did not *understand* this at first: but when Jesus was glorified, then they remembered that this had been written of him and had been done to him (12:16).[1]

In writing in this vein the author means us to understand that it was the disciples' experience of the Holy Spirit after the glorification of Jesus (7:39) which enabled them to "remember" (14:26) and to "understand"

(16:13-15) what Jesus had said and done while he was with them. Moreover, in the absence of Jesus, this group would need to be kept true to his word in what would be, for them, a situation of conflict and hostility (16:1-4; 17:11-17).

In summary, the "we" of John 21:24 who know that the testimony of the beloved disciple is true, are those disciples who were with Jesus, witnessing his signs and beholding his glory, and who, since his glorification, have entered into a deep understanding of Jesus through the activity of the Holy Spirit in the context of opposition and suffering. The beloved disciple speaks as one of them; they confirm the truth of what he says. There is, significantly, the same interplay between individual and group in the first letter of John. On the one hand it states "*we* are writing this" (1:4) while on the other "*I* am writing this" (2:1). Our conclusion is that both the gospel and first letter of John were written by an individual who was a member of a close-knit group which he represented and for which he spoke.

Who is the disciple whom Jesus loved?

The author of this book, "the disciple whom Jesus loved", does not directly disclose his identity. Evidently he was so well known in his circle that he did not need to give his name. Nevertheless, there are three clues in the text which assist us to identify him.

First, he was an intimate friend of Jesus. He was "one of his disciples" who was "lying close to the breast of Jesus" with Peter nearby, perhaps on the other side next to Jesus (John 13:23,24). This disciple also stood with Mary, the mother of Jesus, near the cross. Such was the confidence of Jesus in the man, that he was henceforth to enjoy a son-mother relationship with Mary in his own home (John 19:26-27).

Second, he was a close colleague of Peter. This disciple accompanied Peter on Easter morning to check the story of Mary Magdalene that the stone had been removed from the entrance to the tomb (John 20:2). The discussion by the Sea of Tiberias indicates that he was a close friend both of Jesus and Simon Peter (John 21:20,21).

Third, the "disciple whom Jesus loved" was one of the group of seven disciples by the Sea of Tiberias comprising:

> Simon Peter, Thomas called the Twin, Nathanael of Cana in Galilee, the sons of Zebedee and two others of his disciples (John 21:2).

Since the "disciple whom Jesus loved" was an intimate friend of Jesus and a close colleague of Peter, the most likely candidate is one of "the sons of Zebedee". Because James Zebedee was martyred c.AD 43 (Acts 12:2), the logical conclusion has been to identify this anonymous disciple with John Zebedee. The probability is strengthened by complete absence of any reference to the name "John" in this gospel, except for John the Baptist. Similarly the word "Zebedee" occurs in this book only in the passage quoted.

The earliest list of the New Testament books, the Muratorian Fragment, which is dated c.180–200 states:

> "The fourth book of the gospel is that of John, one of the disciples". Irenaeus, who was a second century writer and a pupil of Polycarp who learned from John Zebedee, wrote:[2]

> Lastly John, the disciple of the Lord, who had leant back on his breast, once more set forth the gospel, while residing at Ephesus in Asia.

The opinion of second century Christian authors is clear. "The disciple whom Jesus loved" was John Zebedee and he wrote the fourth gospel. As we shall see, however, many modern scholars do not agree.

What kind of book?

What kind of document is it that John has written and

why did he write it? Since this is the scripture that many modern evangelists say should be read first, we assume that it is evangelistic in character. But is it? What does the author himself say?

> Now Jesus did many other signs in the presence of his disciples, which are not written in this book; but these are written that you may believe that Jesus is the Christ, the Son of God, and that believing you may have life in his name (John 20:30,31).

The words translated here as "you may believe" do not in the original have the meaning "come to believe" but "go on believing".[3] What John has written, therefore, is not primarily an evangelistic tract designed for people to come to believe *in* Jesus. (He never refers to what he has written as a "gospel".) It is a "book" written to assist Christian readers to "continue" believing that Jesus is the Messiah, the Son of God.

The author does not need to tell the basic gospel story again; his readers, apparently, already know it. Their need was for a clearer and stronger understanding of who Jesus was. In order to help them, the writer, having considered the many miracle signs of Jesus, chose seven to demonstrate the true identity of Jesus. These miracle signs are:

> The turning of water to wine at Cana (John 2:1-11);
> The healing of the son of the nobleman in Capernaum (4:46-54);
> The healing of the cripple at the pool in Jerusalem (5:1-9);
> The feeding of the multitude in the wilderness (6:1-15);
> The healing of the blind man in Jerusalem (9:1-8);
> The raising of Lazarus from the dead in Bethany (11:1-44);
> The resurrection of Jesus himself in Jerusalem (20:1-29).

Why did John select these miracles rather than others? One reason may be that they are so unambiguously miraculous. As we reflect on these seven incidents, there is simply no other interpretation possible. In each case, a great miracle has occurred. *Six hundred and eighty litres* of water were made wine; the boy was healed *from a distance*; the man had been crippled for *thirty-eight years*; *five thousand* men were fed; the man was *born blind*; Lazarus had been buried for *four days* and Jesus for *three*. Such incidents could not be ascribed to imagination or psychic power! A further reason is that several of the miracles appear to be selected to help the readers decide to give up their allegiance to Judaism and to commit all to Jesus. The water that Jesus made into wine had been used for "Jewish rites of purification" (2:6). The miracle of the loaves and fishes provided an opportunity for Jesus to describe himself as the "true bread" (6:32,33), as compared with the "manna in the wilderness" (6:31). These "signs" demonstrate that the old covenant is fulfilled in and ended by Jesus, so that further involvement in Judaism is now pointless.

The author, therefore, is using these miracles, and what Jesus says about them, to argue a case as a lawyer might, to persuade the readers of the rightness of what he is saying. He is not, therefore, writing a history or a biography of Jesus as such, but is attempting to strengthen in his readers a particular view of Jesus. The question for us is: does he use *historical* information in arguing that case? The answer is that the data contained in this book is historical in character and that, of the four evangelists, this writer gives us more specifically historical information than the other three. Let us consider three kinds of historical data in the fourth gospel.

1 Buildings and landscape

The author refers many times to buildings and places in Palestine. As these have been progressively subjected to investigation, there has emerged a healthy respect for the author's knowledge and accuracy of these matters. Let us consider four examples.

(a) John 4:4,11,19

He had to pass through Samaria. So he came to a city of Samaria called Synchar, near the field that Jacob gave to his son, Joseph. Jacob's well was there... "the well is deep"...the [Samaritan] woman said to him..."our fathers worshipped on this mountain ..."

There is a very deep well—approximately forty metres deep—a few hundred metres from the traditional site of Joseph's tomb from which Mt Gerizim, the sacred mountain of the Samaritans, can be seen. Approximately one kilometre to the north of the well is a village called 'Askar which was apparently known as Sychar in the fourth century.[4] Also, the Talmud twice refers to a spring called "'Ain Soker" which may be identical with the fountain in the well near 'Askar. Clearly the Talmud's "Soker" resembles John's "Sychar". The writer, apparently, was familiar with this well.

(b) John 4:46,49,51

So he came again to Cana in Galilee...and at Capernaum there was an official whose son was ill...he went and begged him to *come down* and heal his son..."Sir, *come down* before my child dies"... As he *was going down*, his servants met him...[1]

The threefold reference to "down" is a detail easy to miss, buried as it is within the narrative. The Cana of John's gospel has been identified with Khirbet Qana, which is approximately fifteen kilometres from Nazareth. It is significant that between Cana, where Jesus talked to the official, and Capernaum, where the official's son was the land falls from well above sea level to two hundred metres below sea level, a drop of many hundred metres. The writer has shown, in this narrative, an accurate understanding of the topography of western Galilee.

(c) John 5:2

There is in Jerusalem, by the sheep gate, a pool, in

Hebrew called Bethesda, which has five porticoes.

The archaeologist's spade has laid bare a double pool surrounded by four porticoes, with a fifth on a rock gangway between the two pools. The pool was approximately sixteen metres deep, making it necessary for a crippled person not only to be assisted to the water, but also supported in it. It is not doubted that this is the site described by John.

(d) John 10:22,23

It was the feast of the Dedication at Jerusalem; it was winter and Jesus was walking in the temple, in the portico of Solomon.

Here is a piece of incidental information upon which nothing in the narrative depends. The Maccabean feast of Dedication occurs in winter, just as Christmas in Australia occurs in mid-summer. Jesus seeks shelter from the weather in a particular place, Solomon's porch, which is part of the temple of Herod. If someone wrote of a person seeking shelter from the sun on Christmas day in the Bennelong restaurant in the Sydney Opera House, it would be reasonable to conclude that he had first-hand knowledge of the Australian climate and of a Sydney landmark in the period after the year 1973 when the Opera House was completed. We conclude that the author of this gospel had first-hand understanding of the climate of Judaea and of the architecture of the temple in the period before AD 70 when it was destroyed.

Finally we may note that the fourth evangelist mentions as many as twelve places not referred to in the other gospels. In this regard two experts in the archeology of Palestine have noted that

it is...the single most intensely "theological" or "symbolic" treatise of the New Testament, namely the gospel of John, that is peppered with side references to the geography of Palestine.

Some of these places—"this mountain" [Gerizim] (John 4:20), the Pool of Siloam (9:7) and the Kidron valley (18:1)—are able to be located precisely. Even if all do not have certain identification there is, nevertheless, an air of authenticity in the author's manner of description. He wrote of "Bethany beyond Jordan" (1:28), "Cana in Galilee" (2:1; 4:46)—thereby distinguishing it from Cana in Sidon; "Aenon near Salim... much water there" (3:23); "Ephraim...a town...near the wilderness" (11:54); "a place called The Pavement, and in Hebrew, Gabbatha" (19:13). The qualifying phrases accompanying these place-names strengthen the impression that they are precise geographical locations.[5]

It is this author who records the question of Nathanael: "Can anything good come out of Nazareth?" (1:46) which is, to most readers, fairly meaningless. Similarly, near the end of the gospel, it seems of little account to read that Nathanael is from Cana (21:2). What archaeologists have discovered, however, is that the village they have identified as Cana is quite close to Nazareth. It looks as though Nathanael's sarcastic question is a local proverb about a nearby village which, it now transpires, was very small and off the beaten track. The archaeological evidence is that the author had minute local knowledge which, however, he discloses in quite inconspicuous ways.

The evangelist knows that it is two days' journey from Bethany beyond Jordan (1:28,35,43; 2:1) to Cana, one day from Cana to Capernaum (4:52) and two days from Bethany beyond Jordan to Bethany near Jerusalem (10:40 to 11:18).[6]

It is difficult to escape the conclusion that the fourth evangelist was quite familiar with the topography and buildings of southern Palestine. Meyers and Strange comment that

These examples could be multiplied many times and supplemented with examples of lore, customs and other bits of information known to the author of this gospel. The point we wish to make, however, is simply that an unprejudiced reading of the gospel of John seems to suggest that it is in fact based on a historical and geographical tradition, though not one that simply repeats information from the synoptics.[7]

2 Consistency with the historical context

The Jewish historian Josephus referred to the war between the Jews and Romans AD 66–70 in Palestine as:

> the greatest not only of the wars of our own time, but, so far as accounts have reached us, well nigh of all that ever broke out between cities or nations.[8]

This war separated the history before it from subsequent history in the way a massive freeway cuts a swathe through the countryside and separates one side irreparably from the other.

Tens of thousands of Jews were killed. Hundreds of villages were destroyed and many parts of the landscape denuded of trees.[9] Above all, the temple was destroyed and with it many parts of Jerusalem. All the associated systems—the rosters of priests, the provision of sacrificial animals—were no more. Gone were the chief priests and the infrastructure provided by the Sanhedrin. Judaea came under a more direct Roman military rule. The Sadducean party disappeared and also various rebel factions like the Zealots and the Sicarii. The more extreme Pharisaic party, the Shammaites, passed out of existence, leaving only the benign Hillelites.

Life was as radically different for the Jews after that war in Judaea as it was for the Russians after the 1917 revolution, when the régime of the Czars was replaced by that of Lenin and the Communists. The point is that the fourth evangelist not only does not hint that such a catastrophic war had occurred, but his story is told in terms of what life was like before, not after, that war. In the narrative, and quite innocently, certain Jews comment that it has "taken forty-six years to build this temple" (2:20). In another place the writer comments:

> Now there is in Jerusalem by the sheep gate a pool. . . which has five porticoes (5:2).

It is natural to infer from the present tense of the verb "is" that both buildings were still standing at the time of writing.

C.H. Dodd was struck by the trial narrative in John and the relationship reflected there between the Roman governor and the high priestly leaders:

> It is pervaded with a lively sense for the situation as it was in the last half-century before the extinction of Judaean local autonomy. It is aware of the delicate relations between the native and imperial authorities... These conditions were present in Judaea before AD 70, and not later and not elsewhere.[10]

While Dodd regards the final writer of the gospel as well removed in time and place from his excellent pre-70 sources, J.A.T. Robinson regards it as much more likely that the primitive source and the final writer is one and the same person.[11] It is surely more logical to believe that the gospel was written in the period which it purports to describe, that is before 66. After AD 70, life in Palestine was so different that it would not be possible for someone unfamiliar with the earlier period to have described accurately from his imagination, Jesus at the Feast of Dedication (winter time) walking in Solomon's portico in the temple at Jerusalem.

3 People

The fourth evangelist also shows that his presentation is rooted in history by the references he makes to people. What is interesting is that the information conveyed by this writer has not been derived from the other gospels. Yet there is no reason to doubt the authenticity of this information. Let us consider six people.

(a) John the Baptist

The fourth evangelist alone specifies the places where John the Baptist baptized—"Bethany beyond Jordan" (1:28) and "Aenon near Salim" (3:23). Only this writer informs us that John the Baptist had "disciples" (1:35; 3:25) and that two of these subsequently formed the nucleus of Jesus' disciples (1:35–42). This evangelist alone tells us that Jesus and John, with their respective groups of followers, operated in parallel for some time before John was imprisoned (3:22–24), and that the disciples of Jesus baptized people into their group, in fact more than John the Baptist did into his group (3:22; 4:1–2). If we possessed only the synoptic gospels we would assume that Jesus' public ministry began when John's was finished (Mark 1:14 and parallels) whereas the fourth gospel shows us that, for a period at least, the two ministries overlapped. The statement, found only in this gospel, that "John did no sign" (10:41), is consistent with other evidence about John the Baptist. As an historical source for John the Baptist, we conclude that this gospel contains more detailed information than the synoptic gospels.

(b) Nathanael

Nathanael is mentioned only by the evangelist John, though it is possible that he is, in fact, Nathanael bar Tholomew (Son of Tholomew).[12] He was from Cana in Galilee (21:2) and was known to Philip of Bethsaida, which was also the home town of Andrew and Peter (1:44,45). Though sceptical of any good thing, least of all the Messiah, emanating from nearby Nazareth, he subsequently acknowledged Jesus as "King of Israel" (1:46–49). Nathanael was one of seven persons to whom the risen Jesus revealed himself in Galilee (21:1,2). Everything John tells us of this man—his town of origin, his associations with other Galileans, his sarcastic proverb about Nazareth—suggests authentic historical information.

(c) Joseph

In the synoptic gospels Joseph is mentioned only at the time of the conception and birth of Jesus, that is in about

7 BC. From these sources it would be easy to conclude that Joseph had died some time after the birth of his other children (Mark 6:3) and the commencement of Jesus' public ministry C.AD 29. The gospel of John, however, makes it quite clear that Joseph was alive at the time Jesus fed the multitudes in the wilderness (6.42).[13] Had John depended for his information on the synoptics it is unlikely Joseph would have been mentioned at all.

In both of John's references Jesus is spoken of as "the son of Joseph" (1:45; 6:42) which is the way Jesus' Galilean contemporaries would have referred to him. Later, however, Jesus was said to be "born of a woman", a statement which both believers and opponents used, though for different reasons. Paul, the believer, meant to imply that the conception of Jesus was, by an act of God, without sexual intercourse, whereas Rabbi Eliezer, an opponent, was giving expression to later Jewish propaganda that Jesus was a bastard, born out of wedlock. John's reference to Jesus as "son of Joseph" may be a very early Galilean tradition. Again, the evidence from John, in this case relating to Jesus "son of Joseph", who was alive during the public ministry of Jesus, has all the marks of authenticity and historicity.

(d) Nicodemus

Nicodemus, who is referred to only by this evangelist, appears three times within the narrative. On the first occasion, in Jerusalem (3:1–15), he acknowledges that Jesus is a miracle worker and teacher. In the course of the narrative it emerges that Nicodemus is a member of the sect of the Pharisees (3:1) and indeed a leading rabbi (3:10) and further, that he was a "ruler" (3:1) or member of the Jewish senate, the Sanhedrin.

On the second occasion, also in Jerusalem (7:50) he speaks as "one of them", that is, as belonging to the "rulers" and "Pharisees" (7:48), thus confirming what is stated in the first passage.

The third occasion, again in Jerusalem (19:38,39),

Nicodemus appears with Joseph of Arimathea to collect the body of Jesus. The quantity, one hundred pounds weight (approximately forty-five kg) of mixed myrrh and aloes brought by Nicodemus to apply to the body, is generous but not outlandish. The implication is that this Pharisaic rabbi and Sanhedrin member was also wealthy.

John's information about Nicodemus is detailed, consistent and soberly related without any trace of romanticism. There is no reason to doubt the authenticity of Nicodemus.

(e) Caiaphas

Caiaphas is mentioned twice by Matthew, once by Luke, once in Acts, five times by John and not at all by Mark. From Matthew we learn that Caiaphas was high priest of the Sanhedrin (26:3,57) at the time of the crucifixion, which is in line with Josephus' chronology.[14] Luke, however, refers to the "high priesthood" of Annas *and* Caiaphas (Luke 3:2; cf. Acts 4:6). This is curious, since Annas' high priesthood ended AD 15. Of the various sources of information about Caiaphas, John alone tells us that he was the son-in-law of Annas (John 18:13), which may explain why the two names were linked by Luke as they are also by John (John 18:13,24). Twice John states that "Caiaphas was high priest that year" (John 11:49; 18:13), indicating, perhaps, that Annas retained the real power even after he was deposed, possibly delegating it from time to time to his son-in-law. Whatever the precise arrangements were, it is once again from John that the distinctive information emerges.

(f) Pilate

Pontius Pilate, Roman prefect of Judaea (AD 26–36) is referred to extensively in the New Testament, as he is also in the writings of Josephus and Philo. The latter sources, particularly Philo, depict Pilate as ruthless and unscrupulous. Some scholars, therefore, have expressed incredulity at the relative weakness of character of Pilate portrayed in the synoptic accounts (see especially Luke 23:18–25).

Once again it is the fourth evangelist who supplies information which helps explain why Pilate behaved in such an unusual way in his trial of Jesus. It is found in the words of the Jews to Pilate: "If you release this man, you are not Caesar's friend; everyone who makes himself a king sets himself against Caesar" (John 19:12). Pilate owed his appointment as governor of Judaea, not to his aristocratic birth, but to his "friendship" with the Emperor Tiberius. This "friendship" would have been established in terms of contemporary convention by the emperor's deliberate kindness or favour towards Pilate. Absolute loyalty would have been expected in return. The release of a self-proclaimed king in a Roman province, would have been a clear act of disloyalty to one's "friend", the emperor. Thus John alone conveys that it was not Pilate's weakness but the Jews' blackmail which accounted for the governor's uncharacteristic behaviour.[16]

Is the fourth gospel historical in character? The wealth of information relating to places, to the specific context of the pre-AD 70 period and the details about named individuals, require our acknowledgement that this piece of literature is genuinely historical.

Two problems

Few New Testament scholars take account of what is, in my opinion, the clear historical character of the fourth gospel. For many, the historical question is settled in the negative, without further investigation, because of two problems associated with this gospel. These two problems are seen to be so troublesome that scant attention is paid to the substantial historical element in the book.

The first problem is well stated by G. Bornkamm:

The Gospel according to John has so different a

character in comparison with the other three, and is to such a degree the product of a developed theological reflection, that we can only treat it as a secondary source.[17]

It must be admitted that what the author writes is "the product of a developed theological reflection". The book is marked with powerful symbolism, as in the words "it was night" (13:30), the writer's comment on Judas going out to betray Jesus. His love of imagery may be seen also in the repeated use of the "glory" motif associated with the death and resurrection of Jesus (e.g. 12:23 cf. 7:39). This is different from the synoptic accounts, where glory is associated with the Second Coming and where the Transfiguration is, in effect, a preview of his coming splendour. To focus our attention on the glorification of Jesus in his crucifixion and resurrection, John daringly omits the Transfiguration episode.

It does not follow, however, that such symbolism makes John a "secondary" source. There are three reasons why the fourth gospel should not be regarded as "secondary".

(a) Comparison with the few stories common to the synoptics and John indicates that John is not derived from, but is independent of, other sources. Consider, for example, the clearing of the temple in the accounts of Mark and John:

Mark Chapter 11	John Chapter 2
v.15 And he entered the temple and began to drive out those who sold and those who bought in the temple and he overturned the tables of the money-changers and the seats of those who sold pigeons;	v.14 In the temple he found those who were selling oxen and sheep and pigeons, and the money-changers at their business. v.15 And making a whip of cords, he drove them all, with the

v.16 and he would not allow anyone to carry anything through the temple.

v.17 And he taught, and said to them, "Is it not written, 'My house shall be called a house of prayer...' But you have made it a den of robbers".

sheep and oxen, out of the temple; and he poured out the coins of the money-changers and overturned their tables.

v.16 And he told those who sold the pigeons, "Take these things away: You shall not make my Father's house a house of trade".

The basic story is common to both accounts, so that there is little doubt that both are recounting the same incident. Yet there are numerous differences which make it unlikely that John has copied from Mark. For example, John leaves out "those who bought", Jesus overturning "the seats of those who sold pigeons", and "would not allow anyone to carry anything through the temple".

On the other hand, John includes details such as "sheep and oxen", "making a whip of cords" and "he poured out the coins of the money-changers". Add to these omissions and inclusions the different comment made by Jesus in each account, and it appears highly unlikely that either of these accounts has been derived from the other.

The position, in the fourth and the synoptic gospels, of this incident is a puzzle. Unless Jesus cleared the temple on two different occasions, which is not impossible, we have the problem that the synoptics put it at the end and John puts it at the beginning. It may be that this gospel is rather more thematic than chronological at some points, in which case we can accept that it is John who has relocated the incident. Nevertheless, it should be noted that it is, as we have suggested, an independent source, with more explicit information than Mark, and therefore in no sense a secondary source.

(b) The evidence relating to buildings and places, historical context and specific people show that this writer was consciously utilizing historical information. There are many more pieces of specific information in the fourth gospel than in the other gospels. This document is a primary, not a derived or secondary, document.

(c) Comparison with parallel passages in the early second century writer Ignatius, Bishop of Antioch, shows that John was not the very late author many believe him to be. Compare, for example:

Ignatius	John
For it [the Spirit] knoweth whence it cometh and whither it goeth. (*Philadelphians 7:1*)	The wind blows where it wills...but you do not know whence it comes or whither it goes; (*John 3:8*)

Passages such as this indicate that Ignatius knew and used the fourth gospel. Since Ignatius wrote early in the second century, it follows that this gospel was written during the first century and is therefore not demonstrably later than the other gospels.

These three pieces of evidence—the independence from Mark, the many historical details found only in John, and the pre-Ignatian origin of John's gospel—make it clear that it is not a secondary source. Rather it is as primary an historical source as any other within the New Testament.

The presupposition underlying Bornkamm's statement is that a "developed" theology means a theology written later than less developed ones. But one has only to read the early second century Christian literature, such as 1 Clement or the letter of Polycarp, to discover that although written later than the gospel of Mark or Paul's letter to the Galatians, the later theology is in these cases less theologically developed. While it is agreed that the theology of the fourth gospel is "developed", it does not follow that it is in any way diminished historically. It is preferable to regard this gospel as the most developed theologically, and at the same time, the most explicitly historical of the four gospels.

The second problem relates to the expansive style of speech used by Jesus in John's gospel compared with pithy comparisons and parables in the synoptics. It is argued that if Jesus spoke in one style in Matthew, the speaker in John cannot have been Jesus, and that the speeches of Jesus must have been composed by the evangelist. The force of this argument must be recognized, since the style and vocabulary used throughout the fourth gospel are uniform and it is sometimes difficult to say where the words of Jesus end and those of the evangelist commence. This is a real problem; nevertheless, two comments may be made.

(a) The setting of the teachings of Jesus in the fourth gospel is different from the synoptic tradition. In the synoptic gospels it is the Galilean ministry to country folk which is emphasized, whereas in John, Jesus is mostly in Jerusalem either debating with professional rabbis or speaking in private to the disciples.

Jesus obviously possessed excellent communication skills, so that we should not be surprised that he used different styles of speech in different situations. He addressed large crowds in the open but he also spoke privately to individuals indoors. He employed the conventions of the day in preaching on the set text in the synagogue, and he engaged in verbal cut and thrust in debates with the scribes.[18]

In the gospels we observe Jesus speaking prophetically and proverbially, polemically and pastorally. If a modern politician with less ability to communicate is able to alter his style from the party room to the parliament to the public platform to radio talk-back, how much more variation in style might we expect in so skilful a communicator as Jesus?

(b) In John's gospel Jesus says things differently; but

he does not teach different things. In the synoptics, for example, Jesus clearly taught that God was to be related to as "Father". The difference is that there are only twenty such references in all the synoptic sources combined, and more than one hundred in John. In John's gospel Jesus teaches on fewer subjects but with greater deliberation and repetition; the difference is in the style and not the content.

John Zebedee

Implicit in the doubts surrounding the fourth gospel is the unlikelihood that a Galilean fisherman could have written this profound book. Reference is made to the Book of Acts, where Peter and John are said to be "uneducated, common men" (4:13). How could such men write our gospels? Note, however, that this is the perception of the rulers, elders, scribes and chief priests (4:5,6) who were, as professors and judges, members of an intellectual and religious élite. The words "uneducated" and "common" (Greek: *agrammatoi* and *idiōtēs*) do not mean Peter and John were illiterate but that, compared with those who made the observation, they were non-professionals, laymen.

John Zebedee was from a socio-economic class which ran to "hired servants" (Mark 1:20), so that his circumstances may well have been comparable with the family of the prodigal son, which also had hired servants (Luke 15:18,22,26). John himself was not an employed hand but the member of a partnership of fishermen (Luke 5:10). His mother Salome (Mark 15:40 = Matthew 27:56) was one of a group of women who "ministered to [Jesus]" (Mark 15:41), which means, "provided materially" for him. Salome was probably included in Luke's description of the "many" women who "provided for" Jesus and the twelve "out of their means" (Luke 8:3). The mention of Joanna, wife of Chuza, Herod's steward, among these women, may indicate that the Zebedee family were at least "middle class". Further, it is likely that the unnamed disciple who was "known to the high priest" (John 18:15,16) was, in fact, John Zebedee. Reference to him as "another disciple" (18:15) and "the other disciple" (18:16) certainly resembles the "other disciple, the one whom Jesus loved" (20:2). Peter is present with this "other disciple" in both passages, strengthening the likelihood that it is John. Acquaintance with the high priest would imply that this disciple belonged to the middle or upper strata of Jewish society.

By New Testament times, Palestine was to a significant degree Hellenised, with perhaps a majority of middle class persons able to speak both Aramaic and Greek. Based as he was at busy Capernaum in "Galilee of the Gentiles" and belonging to the socio-economic group described, it is reasonable to expect that John Zebedee is bilingual, with Greek as his second language. J.A.T. Robinson commented that the fourth evangelist was a writer "whose first language was evidently Aramaic and who wrote correct, though limited, Greek".[19]

John Zebedee the disciple of Jesus, along with his brother James and Peter, was one of the inner trio. He was one of the first called into Jesus' company (Mark 1:19). In addition to his experience as a member of the twelve, he was a privileged witness to:
    the healing of Peter's mother-in-law (Mark 1:29)
    the raising of the daughter of Jairus (Mark 5:37)
    the transfiguration (Mark 9:2)
    the Olivet discourse (Mark 13:3)
    the testing in Gethsemane (Mark 14:33)
If ever a person was singularly well equipped by experience to write a gospel, it was John Zebedee.

This was not the end. Though younger than his brother James (Mark 1:19), John is given precedence over James after the resurrection (Acts 1:13). It is only John who is regularly mentioned with Peter in the earliest history of Christianity, both in Jerusalem (Acts Chapters 3 and 4) and also in Samaria (Acts 8:14–25). Along with James, brother of Jesus, and Peter, John is mentioned as one of the three "pillars" of the Jerusalem church who took part in the far reaching Missionary Agreement in Jerusalem c.47 (Galatians 2:7–9). In addition to his three years in the fellowship of Jesus, John Zebedee was to act as a leader of the Jerusalem church for approximately fifteen years:

AD 30–33: Disciple of Jesus

AD 33–47: "Pillar" apostle of Jerusalem church

Then, so far as the New Testament is concerned, John Zebedee disappears from view. But there can be little doubt that he had the education and the experience to write the gospel which bears his name.

Two options: true or false

Two connected views about the fourth gospel are expressed by a number of New Testament scholars. On the one hand they reject its authorship by an original disciple while, on the other, they praise literary and theological qualities of his book. R.E. Brown refers to the author as a "master preacher and theologian" who was, nevertheless, "not famous".[20] C.K. Barrett states that "the evangelist" was "perhaps the greatest theologian in all the history of the church" but "was now forgotten. His name was unknown..."[21]

The evidence from the second century is quite the reverse. The author was indeed "famous"; he was John Zebedee. Why is it that some modern scholars balk at the testimony of Irenaeus, whose teacher Polycarp was a pupil of John Zebedee? Why will they not accept the considerable weight of internal evidence which identifies "the disciple whom Jesus loved" with John Zebedee? It is no compensation to lavish praise on their shadowy anonymous author as "the greatest theologian in all history".

There is a deeper issue. Our author states that,
He who saw it has borne *witness*—his testimony is *true*,
and he knows that he tells the *truth*.

(John 19:35)

This author claims to have been a true witness, that is,
an eyewitness, of Jesus. In his first letter he said that he
and his fellows had "heard", "seen" and "touched" the
"word of life" (1 John 1:1-2). His claims are extensive
and specific.

The alternatives are simple. Either the writer was the
truthful eyewitness he claims to have been, or, as Barrett
and Brown believe, he was not. If Barrett and Brown are
correct, the author was not in fact an eyewitness and not
a disciple. Therefore it appears to me that he was not
truthful at this point. If he was not truthful he cannot be
a "great theologian", since theology is about God, who
is truth. Although, according to Barrett and Brown, the
fourth evangelist is "the greatest theologian in history",
he himself does not claim to be a theologian at all; he
simply claims to be a special friend of Jesus and a true
witness to his signs, his crucifixion and his risen person.
The problem of his fundamental claim being incorrect is
not really resolved by praising him at a point where he
makes no claims. What cannot be denied is that all the
evidence on the identity of the author, from both inside
and outside the fourth gospel, points not to an unknown
author but to John Zebedee, the beloved disciple.

Many scholars cannot believe that the fourth gospel could
have been written by a member of Jesus' original circle
of disciples. Their chief difficulty lies with the author's
expansive style of writing and with the sophistication of
his theology. The author, it is claimed, wrote later than
the synoptics and from outside the milieu of Palestine.

In the last decades, however, greater knowledge of the
geography of Palestine, along with the results of archaeological work, has led others to believe that the author was,

in fact, familiar with the countryside of both Galilee and Judaea, and that he had an intimate knowledge of Jerusalem and the temple area.

Greater awareness of the difference in the ethos after the war AD 66–70 has strengthened the case that the author wrote from the earlier, rather than the later, period. This is consistent with the book's own identification of its author as "the beloved disciple" and with the united opinion of second century Christians, that "the beloved disciple" was John Zebedee.

What then of the expansive style and sophisticated theology? How could John Zebedee have been responsible for these? We reply that someone wrote this book and that it was written before the end of the first century. Are there any substantial, as opposed to merely stylistic, grounds, for doubting John Zebedee was that someone? His involvement with Jesus, as one of the inner circle, and his lengthy experience of leadership in the Jerusalem Christian community, add to the strong probability that John Zebedee was in fact the author of the fourth gospel.

Further reading to Chapter Six:
A.M. Hunter, *According to John*, S.C.M., London, 1968.
L.L. Morris, *Studies in the Fourth Gospel*, Paternoster, Exeter, 1969.
J.A.T. Robinson, *Re-dating the New Testament*, S.C.M., London, 1976.
S. Smalley, *John: Evangelist and Interpreter*, Paternoster, Exeter, 1978.

Notes
[1]My italics.

[2]Reported in Eusebius, *Ecclesiastical History*, 5, 8, 4, Tr. G.A. Williamson, (Penguin Classics).

[3]Although both readings occur in ancient manuscripts—the one translated "go on believing" is to be preferred because it occurs in the earliest manuscript and has good support elsewhere.

[4]*See* further, F.F. Bruce, *Places They Knew*, London, 1981, pp.35–38.

[5]E.M. Meyers and J.F. Strange, *Archaeology, the Rabbis and Early Christianity*, London, 1981, p.160.

[6]If, as it appears, the time of the arrival of the news to Jesus coincided with the time of Lazarus' death (11:3 cf. 11:11).

[7]*Op cit.*, p.161.

[8]*The Jewish War* 1:1.

[9]For the Roman siegeworks.

[10]*Historical Tradition in the Fourth Gospel*, C.U.P., 1963, p.120.

[11]Robinson, *Redating The New Testament*, p.297. Many scholars, however, regard John 9:22 as evidence that this Gospel arises out of the post-70 milieu.

[12]*See* Mark 3:18 and parallels.

[13]Jesus' commitment of his mother into the care of "the disciple whom Jesus loved" (John 19:26), suggests that Joseph had died by that time.

[14]*Antiquities*, 18:35,95; cf. 18:64.

[15]Josephus, *Antiquities*, 18:27; cf. 34.

[16]*See* E.A. Judge, *The Social Pattern of the Christian Groups in First Century*, London, 1960, p.34.

[17]*Jesus of Nazareth*, Hodder and Stoughton, London, 1960, p.14.

[18]*See* A.M. Hunter, *According to John*, S.C.M., London, 1968, pp.97–98.

[19]*Redating the New Testament*, p.299.

[20]*The Gospel According to John*, Anchor Bible, New York, 1966–70.

[21]*The Gospel According to St John*, SPCK, London, 1960, p.114.

CHAPTER SEVEN

Witness Two: Peter Through Mark

Although the second gospel does not say who wrote it, Christians of the following century were in no doubt. Their unanimous opinion was that it was written by Mark on the basis of information supplied by Peter. Writing c.130 at Hierapolis in Asia Minor, Papias, "a hearer of John", stated:

Mark...having been the interpreter of Peter, wrote ...all that he recalled of what was either said or done by the Lord. For he neither heard the Lord, nor was he a follower of his, but at a later date...of Peter.[1]

This is also the view of Justin writing in Rome c.150, of Irenaeus in Gaul c.170 and of Clement in Alexandria c.180.

But were Peter and Mark capable of writing the gospel of Mark? Many modern scholars now believe this gospel, despite its apparent simplicity, to be a skilfully written and profound piece of literature. Were humble folk like Peter and Mark capable of creating a document like this?

Peter and John Mark

Was Peter the poor and illiterate person he is often supposed to have been? In fact, he was involved in a fishing partnership (Luke 5:10), and, with his brother Andrew, he owned a house in Capernaum (Mark 1:29).

Since he was a person of at least modest means, he may be assumed to have been literate, as people from his socio-economic class were usually educated to some degree.

Some time after Jesus' resurrection Peter moved to Jerusalem, where for ten years (c.33–43) he was leader of the large Jerusalem Christian community and its spokesman both to the crowds (Acts 2:14–42; 3:12–26), and also to the high priests (Acts 4:8–12; 5:29–32). Doubtless some personal and intellectual development occurred as Peter moved from a fishing business in Capernaum to Jerusalem, the world capital of the Jewish people, where he engaged in such activities as leading, preaching and teaching (Acts 2:40,42; 6:2).

During this period, however, Peter was not confined to Jerusalem; after the killing of Stephen and the scattering of the Christian Hellenists, Peter (with John Zebedee) travelled to Samaria (Acts 8:14–25) to check on and consolidate Philip's evangelism of the Samaritans. Later, he visited Christian groups in Lydda and Joppa (Acts 9:32–43), and probably others in the coastal strip from Azotus to Caesarea where Philip had been active (Acts 8:40). He came, eventually, to Caesarea the Roman garrison city, where Philip had settled (Acts 8:40; 21:8) and spoke in the house of a senior Roman officer, Cornelius (Acts 10:24–48).

In c.43 the leadership of the Jerusalem church passed to James, the Lord's brother, since Peter was forced to flee because of Herod Agrippa's persecutions (Acts 12:1–3,17). Nevertheless, he remained within the orbit of the Jerusalem church, being referred to as one of its "pillars", though by then (c.47), his name was mentioned after that of James (Galatians 2:9).

At the missionary "summit" meeting c.47 (Galatians 2:7–9) it was agreed that Peter, as well as James and John, should go to the Jews with the Christian message. This, apparently is what Peter proceeded to do. We hear of him in Antioch c.49 (Galatians 2:11–14) and in

Corinth c.53 (1 Corinthians 1:12; 9:5). The first letter of Peter appears to have been written from Rome (1 Peter 5:13 "Babylon" = ? Rome) in the early sixties.

Peter's is a remarkable story. He began as an obscure fisherman in remote Capernaum and when last heard of was in Rome, the capital of the Empire. In the intervening three decades he accompanied Jesus in Galilee and Judaea, led the church in Jerusalem, was an itinerant missionary pastor in Palestine, and travelled as a missionary to the Jewish dispersion in Syria, Greece and Italy. Is it really so incredible that someone with this breadth of experience, despite relatively humble origins, should provide the resource information for the second gospel?

What of John Mark? The house of his mother was apparently a major meeting place for the Jerusalem Church, or perhaps that part of it that looked to the leadership of Peter as opposed to James (Acts 12:12-17; cf. Galatians 1:18,19). Reference to "the house of Mary" suggests she was a widow; Mark's father is never mentioned. It was apparently a large house since "many were gathered together...praying" (Acts 12:12). The presence of a maid (Acts 12:13) adds to a picture of a substantial, possibly wealthy, establishment to which John Mark belonged. His two names, John (Hebrew), and Mark (Greek or Latin), together with a probably affluent background, make it likely that this man was educated and bilingual, with Greek as his second language.

John Mark was associated with famous leaders. He was a cousin of Barnabas (Colossians 4:10), whom he accompanied c.50 on what was probably a missionary tour of Cyprus (Acts 15:39). Earlier, c.47, he was the younger colleague of Barnabas and Paul for the first part of the missionary tour of Cyprus and southern Galatia (Acts 13:15). The dispute between Paul and John Mark (Acts 15:37-39) was subsequently resolved, since in the early sixties (?) the apostle refers to him as a "fellow worker" (Philemon 23) and as someone whose help he

needed (2 Timothy 4:11). Peter, writing from Rome
c.63, refers affectionately to Mark as "my son" (1 Peter
5:13), possibly reflecting a surrogate father relationship
going back to Jerusalem in the thirties and forties.

. The gospel which bears Mark's name contains a detail
which, significantly, is found in no other gospel. At the
arrest of Jesus in Jerusalem,

> ...a young man followed him, with nothing but a
> linen cloth about his body; and they sensed him. But
> he left the linen cloth and ran away naked (14:51,52).

This is, according to William Barclay, "an extra-
ordinarily trivial and irrelevant incident to insert into the
high tragedy of the events in the garden".[2] He quotes T.
Zahn: "Mark paints a small picture of himself in the
corner of his work". If Mark was in fact the "young
man" of, shall we say, twenty years of age in the year
c.33, by the early sixties when many suppose him to have
written his gospel he would not have been much short of
fifty years old.

John Mark, then, was from a financially strong background, therefore educated and bilingual. He had been
the close colleague of Barnabas, Paul and Peter, and by
the time he was fifty years of age, had worked as missionary with one or both of them for a decade and a half.

Let us consider one further piece of information. In the
prologue to his two volume work, Luke acknowledges
having received written information about Jesus from
certain "ministers" before him, one of whom must have
been the author of Mark, since so much of his gospel is
incorporated in the gospel according to Luke. The Greek
word for minister is *hypēretēs* which means: "assistant to
another as the instrument of his will" and is a word Luke
used of John Mark on the first missionary tour. Barnabas
and Paul "had John as *hypēretēs*"—as their minister or
attendant. Is Luke identifying John Mark the *hypēretēs*
(Acts 13:5) with the author of a text on which he came to
rely (Luke 1:2)?

Our conclusion is that in terms of education and

experience Peter and John Mark could have written the second gospel, as second century Christian writers claimed. But did they? Unfortunately, as we have seen, this gospel does not state who wrote it, except to imply that the author was the "young man" in Jerusalem who fled naked into the darkness on the night Jesus was arrested. The one course of enquiry open to us is to decide whether or not the information contained in the gospel and its manner of presentation is consistent with Petrine-Marcan authorship. If Peter was the source of the information Mark used, we would expect to discover biographical and historical elements. But do we find them?

Proclamation or history?

"The beginning of the gospel of Jesus Christ, the Son of God"—these are the words with which the second evangelist commenced his scroll and which became its title. What he wrote is a "gospel", the only one of the four we call "gospels" to call itself by that name. Elsewhere in the New Testament the "gospel" is "proclaimed" or "spoken"; this is the only case where it is *written*.

There are a number of summaries of the "proclaimed" gospel in the Acts of the Apostles, as for example when Peter spoke to Cornelius and his family in Caesarea (Acts 10:34–43). The chief points Peter made to them were:

> After the baptism which John the Baptist proclaimed
> God anointed Jesus of Nazareth with power
> So that he proclaimed the gospel, beginning in Galilee
> and throughout all Judaea.
> God was with him as he went about healing all who
> were oppressed by the devil.
> The people of Jerusalem had him crucified
> But God raised him on the third day.

In 1932 C.H. Dodd noticed that this summary of Peter's speech bears a striking resemblance to the sequence and structure of the written "gospel", especially the gospel of Mark. According to Dodd the written gospel was an expanded version of the spoken gospel.

It may be that what the second evangelist wrote was primarily intended to be read aloud to an audience, rather than simply to be read by an individual alone. Is it relevant that two thirds of the episodes in this gospel are less than ten sentences long? Certainly the narrative is fast moving and gripping, with a minimum of recorded speech. One of the most successful postwar London stage shows, and which played nightly to full houses, consisted of a cast of one person whose only script was the text of Mark's gospel. Even though written, does Mark somehow remain "proclamation", intended to arouse our passions and move our wills to believe in Jesus?

There is no way that it could be regarded as a "life of Jesus". The adult Jesus simply enters the story near the beginning and is the focus of attention in the episodes which follow. There is an almost complete absence of such biographical detail as: his father's name, his birth-place, his education, his age or his appearance. The story is told with a high sense of drama, so that although Jesus would have visited Jerusalem for the Jewish feasts nine or ten times during the three-year period of his public life, this evangelist has him going there only once—to die!

Is this gospel, therefore, unbiographical and unhistorical? The answer is that, although it is primarily in the form of a "proclamation", there are also at least four historical elements which characterize the gospel of Mark.

1 Overall historical context

The gospel of Mark permits us to place Jesus within a recognisable historical context. He began his public life in Galilee after the famous prophet *John the Baptist* had been arrested (1:14). His own mission as well as that of his disciples occurred during the period *Herod Antipas* was the tetrarch of Galilee and Peraea (6:14). He was tried by the

Roman Prefect of Judaea, *Pontius Pilate*, and crucified by his decision (15:15). These three persons, serve as historical markers for the ministry of Jesus in the gospel of Mark, because they are well known in other historical sources—John in Josephus, Antipas in Josephus and Tacitus[4] and Pilate in Philo, Josephus and Tacitus.

Mark and Josephus give different names for Herodias' former husband,[5] before she married Antipas (Mark 6:17; *Antiquities* 18:136), but this is a relatively minor detail and does not detract from the overall dovetailing of Mark into a known historical context.

2 The Herodians

The gospel of Mark refers to a group known as the "Herodians",[6] who strongly opposed Jesus in both Galilee and Jerusalem (Mark 3:6; 12:13). Although scholars are uncertain about their exact composition and rationale, their historicity is not in question. It is significant that Mark's gospel is the only primary source of historical information for this group. Matthew's only reference is clearly derived from Mark (Matthew 22:16 = Mark 12:13). The Herodians are not mentioned in Luke or John.

3 Geographical details

The gospel of Mark depicts Jesus as based in Capernaum (see also Matthew 4:13) on the northern shore of Galilee, but mentions that he increasingly needed to withdraw,[7] for various reasons and for apparently more and more lengthy periods, outside Galilee. While this is not made obvious by the author, careful reading makes it likely to have been the case.

After his initial and spectacular activities in Capernaum (1:28,33) Jesus withdrew because of the crowds (1:37,38) to "all Galilee, preaching in their synagogues" (1:39).

Back in Capernaum (2:1) it became necessary to leave on account of the Pharisees' and Herodians' plot (3:6).

He engaged in public ministry by the Sea of Galilee (3:7) and went to an unidentified mountain for intensive teaching of the twelve (3:13).

Again in Capernaum (3:19), after a dispute with scribes from Jerusalem, he withdrew to the seaside for public teaching (3:22-30). He stayed in the boat from which he had been speaking and travelled direct to the Decapolis (4:1,35,36; 5:1). After they recrossed the sea to the town where Jairus lived (5:21-43), he visited Nazareth (6:1-6a) and then visited the villages of Galilee (6:6b).

When Jesus returned to Capernaum (6:7), he dispatched the twelve for their village mission; they returned to him (6:30), followed by men from "all the towns" (6:33), their mission having come to the attention of Herod Antipas (6:14). Again he withdrew, with them, to the north-east side of the lake at or near Bethsaida (see Luke 9:10) where the people sought to make him king (see John 6:14,15).

Jesus is next found at Gennesaret in Galilee (6:53) whence he returned to Capernaum, and became involved in a serious dispute with local (?) Pharisees and Jerusalem scribes (7:1). Once more he left, and this time went to the districts of Tyre and Sidon on the distant coast of Phoenicia (7:24), and from there to the region of Decapolis (7:31), where he fed the four thousand (8:1-9).

Jesus' next visit to Galilee was brief. When he and the disciples went from the Decapolis to Dalmanutha (8:10), there was yet another dispute with the Pharisees (8:11,12) so they left immediately by boat (8:13) for Bethsaida (8:22), with Jesus warning the disciples of the "leaven of the Pharisees and...of Herod [Antipas]" (8:15), the two sources of opposition which kept forcing him out of Galilee. From Bethsaida they travelled to the northern and mountainous regions of Caesarea Philippi (8:27), near the source of the Jordan. Six days after Peter had declared Jesus to be "the Christ" (8:29), Jesus took three of the disciples to a "high mountain", (probably Mt.

Hermon, almost three thousand metres high and about twenty kilometres north-east of Caesarea Philippi), where the transfiguration occurred (9:2–8). From there they set out for Jerusalem, re-entering Galilee, but in great secrecy (9:30), and returning to "the house" in Capernaum (9:33). Jesus and the twelve then followed the Jordan valley (10:1), coming eventually to Jericho (10:46) and ultimately to Jerusalem (11:1, 11).

Thus the gospel of Mark does convey a strong sense of extensive activity in Galilee, based in Capernaum but with periods of enforced withdrawal to neighbouring regions to the west, east and north. Mark's account, told in terms of the persistent opposition of local and Judaean Pharisees and with the ever-present menace of the tetrarch Herod Antipas (and the "Herodians"), is expressed in terms of specific geographic movement inside and outside Galilee, and is therefore quite historically credible.

4 Linkages between episodes

The gospel of Mark, despite the claims of some scholars that it is a haphazard collection of episodes with no developing story, does in fact contain a number of biographical and historical links between the episodes.

One example is the "house" in Capernaum which belonged to Simon (and his brother Andrew?) to which Jesus came (1:29) and where he initially stayed (1:33, 35–36). It was to this "house" that he returned after his various voluntary and enforced withdrawals from Capernaum (2:1, 3:19; [?7:17;] 9:33). Evidently this house became his own home and his base of operations for ministry in greater Galilee and the regions outside Galilee.[8] These Capernaum "house" references, which span the various episodes for more than half the gospel, are an indication that, in an overall way, the gospel of Mark is historical in character.

Another example is Jesus' relationship with people in another town, his own town, Nazareth. He left Nazareth to be baptized by John in the Jordan (1:9) some time after which he settled in Capernaum (1:29 cf. Matthew 4:13). He is regularly referred to as "Jesus of Nazareth" (1:24, 10:47; 16:6) or as "the Nazarene, Jesus" (14:67). Apart from his visit to Nazareth after his baptism (Luke 4:16–30), he appears not to have returned there for some time. When he came back, the people of Nazareth were so sceptical (Mark 6:2) that he made his famous remark that "a prophet is not without honour" (6:4). Those however, who did not "honour" this prophet were those of "his own country" (district or region), "his own kin" (extended family) and "his own house" (immediate family as in 6:3—Mary his mother, his brothers James, Joses, Judas, and Simon and his sisters, who are not mentioned by name). The scepticism of Nazareth was thoroughgoing, extending from his immediate family through the network of relatives to the wider community.

This scepticism in Nazareth was not new. Earlier "his family" (3:21), that is his mother and brothers (3:31), set out from Nazareth to Capernaum to "seize" him (3:21) since they believed he was "out of his mind" (3:21). On arrival they stood "outside" (3:31), presumably outside the house in Capernaum, whereupon Jesus commented that his (true) mother and brothers were those who did the will of God (3:35).

Here then is another linkage, spanning four chapters, indicating the consistent unbelief of the people of Nazareth, including his own family, as contrasted with the new "family" in Capernaum, based as it was on the house of Simon and Andrew. These two intersecting examples of references which span several episodes and chapters are evidence of the underlying historicity of the gospel of Mark.

In conclusion we ask: does the written proclamation also have biographical and historical characteristics which would be consistent with Petrine-Marcan authorship? The evidence for an affirmative answer is that Mark's story dovetails into its historical context; that it refers to the existence of the "Herodians" group; that Jesus' withdrawals are consistent with the historical circumstances of Galilee and with its geography; and that certain subtle linkages between episodes imply that the narrative is founded on historical truth.

But is there more that can be said?

Evidence of an eyewitness

In this section we will attempt to show that, in addition to information of an historical character, there are also traces of evidence which in all probability go back to an eyewitness.

1 Vivid detail

There are many examples of vivid detail in the gospel of Mark. Where do they come from? Do they arise from the author's lively imagination or from his recollection of things which made an impression on his memory? If the examples were long descriptive passages we would be inclined to attribute them to his imagination. Since, however, they are confined to small details it is more likely that they arose from his recollection of striking and colourful events. Let us consider some examples.

(a) That evening, at *sundown...the whole city* was gathered together about [literally "facing"] *the door* (1.32,33).[8]

The expectancy of the crowd facing the door at sundown has impressed the memory of an eye witness. How else do we explain these words?

(b) ...when *evening* had come...leaving the crowd, they took him with them in the boat, *just as he was*. And *other boats* were with him...and the waves beat into the boat, so that *the boat was already filling*. But he was in the *stern, asleep on the cushion*, (4:35-38).[9]

This passage reflects the emotions of horror and fear that Jesus was asleep when the boat was filling with water.

(c) ...a man...who lived among the tombs...had often been bound with fetters and chains, but the chains he *wrenched apart*, and the fetters he *broke in pieces*; and no one had the strength to subdue him. Night and day among the tombs and on the mountains he was always *crying out*, and *bruising* himself *with stones* (5:2-5).[9]

Here is a grim picture of chains hanging from hands and legs and the bruised body as well as of the reports of weird nocturnal noises which imprinted itself upon the memory of someone who had been present.

(d) When they came to the house of the ruler of the synagogue, he *saw a tumult*, and people *weeping and wailing loudly*...he said to them "...The child is not dead but sleeping." And they *laughed at him*...Taking her by the hand he said to her, "*Talitha cumi*" (5:38-41).[9]

The Aramaic words stand out against the memory of the sounds of wailing and scornful laughter as the very words used by Jesus to the dead child.

(e) He commanded them all to sit down by companies upon the *green grass*. So the people sat down in *groups* [literally as "garden beds"] by *hundreds* and by *fifties* (6:39,40).[9]

This is almost a photographic image of people sitting in groups, their colourful robes giving the appearance of flower beds set in green grass.

These words of Mark leap from the page. To my mind they can only have come from the memory of someone who was struck by the drama of the scene or its colour, or sound or strangeness. Behind these words are the recollections of someone who had been present.

2 The emotions of Jesus

Prominent among the vivid details in Mark's gospel are the emotional and personal responses of Jesus in particular situations. Again, we ask: How do we account for these in the gospel? Are they the result of the author's imagination or of his recollection? They are not system-atically developed by the author and there is no sign that they have been contrived in any way. Rather, they are mentioned by the writer in passing. Let us examine some examples.

(a) A leper came to him...*moved with pity* [Jesus] stretched out his hand and touched him...and he *sternly* charged him and sent him away (1:40-43).[9]

(b) ...a man was there who had a withered hand. And they watched...whether he would heal him on the sabbath...And he looked around at them with *anger*, *grieved* at their hardness of heart, and said to the man, "Stretch our your hand." (3:1,2,5).[9]

(c) The apostles returned to Jesus...And *he said* to them, "*Come away by yourselves to a lonely place, and rest a while*"...As he went ashore he saw a great throng, and he had *compassion* on them, because they were like sheep without a shepherd; (6:30-34).[9]

(d) Immediately he *made* [= compelled] his disciples get into the boat and go before him to the other side... (6:45).[9]

(e) And they were bringing children to him, that he might touch them; and the disciples rebuked them. But when Jesus saw it he was *indignant*, and said to them, "Let the children come to me..." And he took them in his arms and blessed them, laying his hands upon them (10:13-16).[9]

(f) ...a man ran up and knelt before him, and asked ...And Jesus looking upon him *loved* him... (10:17,21).[9]

(g) And he took with him Peter and James and John, and began to be greatly *distressed and troubled*. And he said..."My soul is very sorrowful, even to death..." (14:33,34).[9]

(h) "Elo-i, Elo-i, lama sabach-thani?" which means "My God, my God, why has thou *forsaken* me?" (15:34).[9]

How else do we explain these references to the

intensely human and emotional behaviour of Jesus, his compassion, his anger, his fatigue, his concern for others, his indignation, his love, his dread, his sense of abandonment—except as reactions which registered strongly with someone who was present at the time. It seems unlikely that such references arose out of an author's imagination.

On five occasions this author mentions that Jesus "looked around" (as in a circle): in the synagogue when they watched if he would heal on the Sabbath (3:5); in the house in Capernaum with his mother and brothers outside (3:34); at the crowd, to see who touched him (5:32); to the disciples when he said how hard it was for the wealthy to enter the kingdom of God (10:23); and on his arrival in the temple (11:11). This "look", which occurred on dramatic occasions, is not recorded by Matthew and only once by Luke. Underlying Mark's account is the memory of someone who saw, and was deeply impressed by, the way Jesus "looked around" at these times of high drama.

3 "They" passages

In 1928 C.H. Turner, in his commentary on Mark, noticed that the second evangelist often used "they" in his narrative, speaking of the disciples, whereas Matthew and Luke frequently omit them, referring only to Jesus and the other person in the story. Mindful of Papias' statement that Mark wrote what he heard from Peter, Turner suggested that Peter must have often said "we", speaking for himself and the other disciples present with Jesus. Since Mark was not present with Peter and the others, he cannot write "we"; he must write "they". When Matthew and Luke take over Mark's material the word "they" drops out, leaving the singular "he", Jesus. Thus, in Turner's reconstruction, the process was:

Peter's teaching →	Marks' writing →	Matthew and
of component	of component	Luke supple-
stories	stories	menting and
		adapting Mark

We + Jesus +	*They* + Jesus	Jesus +
person(s) in	+ person(s) in	person(s) in
story	story	story

There are many of Mark's stories in which we can easily imagine the "they" having originally been, from Peter's mouth, "we"; for example:

And immediately he left the synagogue and entered the house of Simon and Andrew, with James and John... Simon's [my] mother-in-law lay sick with a fever, and immediately they [we] told him of her. And he came and took her by the hand... (1:29–31).

Note that Matthew (8:14ff) has removed all plurals while Luke (4:38ff) has altered two of the three plurals. Other examples in Mark's gospel are:

And they [we] came to Bethsaida. And some people brought to him a blind man... (8:22).

They [we] went on from there and passed through Galilee. And he would not have any one know it; (9:30).

And they [we] came to Jerusalem. And he entered the temple... (11:15).

Whilst it is not possible to prove Papias' statement that Mark was the "interpreter of Peter", (a statement with which every second century writer who ventures an opinion on the authorship of the second gospel agrees), the internal evidence is quite consistent with that statement. Whilst the C.H. Turner view must remain as no

more than an interesting possibility, it seems to me that
the vivid details and the references to the emotions of
Jesus demand that behind the written text lies the testimony of an eyewitness.

Jesus in Jerusalem

Although the gospel of Mark has sixteen chapters, no less
than six are devoted to what happened to Jesus in Jerusalem. In terms of actual words, Mark devotes approximately one third of his gospel to the events of those few
days in Jerusalem. It may be significant that these
chapters are very precise and detailed in matters of *time*,
place and *people*.

1 Details of time
   And he entered Jerusalem, and went into the
   temple...it was already *late*... (11:11)
   On the *following day*... (11:12)
   As they passed by *in the morning*... (11:20)
   And they came again to Jerusalem. (11:27)
   It was not *two days* before the Passover... (14:1)
   And on the *first day* of Unleavened Bread... (14:12)
   And when *it was evening*... (14:17)
   And as soon as it *was morning*... (15:1)
   And it was the *third* hour... (15:25)
   And when the *sixth* hour had come... (15:33)
   And when *evening* had come... (15:42)
   And when the *sabbath was past*... (16:1)[9]

2 Details of place
   ...they drew near to *Jerusalem*, to *Bethphage and
   Bethany*, at the *Mount of Olives*... (11:1 cf. 11:15, 27;
   14:16)
   ...he went out to *Bethany*... (11:11 cf. 14:3)
   And as he came out of the *temple*... (13:1)
   And as he sat on the *Mount of Olives* opposite the temple
   ... (13:3 cf. 14:26)

And they went to a place which was called *Gethsemane*; (14:32)
And Peter had followed him at a distance, right into *the courtyard of the high priest*; (14:54)
And the soldiers led him away inside the *palace* (that is, the *praetorium*). (15:16)
And they brought him to the place called *Golgotha*...
And they crucified him... (15:22,24)
And he [Joseph of Arimathea] laid him in a [his] *tomb* which had been hewn out of the rock; (15:46)[9]

3 Details of people

Apart from those disciples who are named and the Roman prefect, Pontius Pilate, Mark mentions the following by name: Barabbas, a murderer who had taken part in "the insurrection" (15:6–15); "Simon of Cyrene", "the father of Alexander and Rufus" (15:21); "Mary Magdalene" also "Mary the mother of James the younger and of Joses", and "Salome" (15:40; 16:1) and "Joseph of Arimathea" (15:43ff).

Since there are so many details in those last six chapters, it has been suggested that they originally existed separately as the earliest part of the gospel to assume written form. This part of Mark's gospel refers five times to the "high priest" (14:53, 54, 60, 61, 63) without mentioning his name. This has been taken to imply that Caiaphas was still the high priest when the story was being written, there being no need to mention his name. Since Caiaphas was high priest until AD 37, it is possible that this Jerusalem gospel came into being before that date.

As to the author, we conjecture that if Peter was at that stage associated with the home of John Mark (see Acts 12:12–17) it is quite possible that this part of the gospel arose from the collaborative effort of Peter and Mark back in the middle thirties.

Upon examination, the gospel of Mark is found to be consistent with the statement of Papias that Mark used Peter as his source. Looked at as a whole, this gospel corresponds with Peter's preaching outline as in the speech to Cornelius. Considered in its component parts, it is found to be rich in historical information and vivid detail, supporting the proposition that an eyewitness wrote, or was the source of, the gospel of Mark.

Further reading to Chapter Seven:
W. Barclay, *The Gospels and Acts* vol. 1, S.C.M., London, 1976.
C.H. Dodd, *The Apostolic Preaching and its Developments*, Hodder & Stoughton, London, 1960.
R.P. Martin, *Mark—Evangelist and Theologian*, Paternoster, Exeter, 1972.
H. Straudinger, *The Trustworthiness of the Gospels*, E.T. Handsell Press, Edinburgh, 1981.

Notes
[1] Quoted in Eusebius *H.E.*, 3:39.

[2] *The Gospels and Acts* vol. 1, SCM, London, 1976, p.116.

[3] I.G. Kittel, *Theological Dictionary of the New Testament*, E.T. Grand Rapids, 1972, Vol. 8, p.539.

[4] *Histories* 5:9 (Antipas is not actually mentioned by name).

[5] See further H. Hoehner, *Herod Antipas*, Grand Rapids, 1980, pp.131–136.

[6] *Ibid.*, pp.331–342.

[7] *Ibid.*, pp.317–330.

[8] For discussion about the discovery of the house of Peter in Capernaum *see* Meyers & Strange, *Archaeology, the Rabbis and Early Christianity*, pp.59–60, 128–130.

[9] My italics.

CHAPTER EIGHT

Luke and Matthew

Now that we have discussed the gospels by John and Mark, we turn to the two remaining evangelists, Luke and Matthew.

Luke
From the second half of the second century Christian writers are unanimous about two matters.

First, they attribute the third gospel to Luke, the physician who accompanied Paul on his journeys.
Thus the Muratorian Canon written from Rome c.190 states:

> The third book of the gospel, that according to Luke, was compiled in his own name on Paul's authority by Luke the Physician, when after Christ's ascension Paul had taken him to be with him...yet neither did he see the Lord in the flesh...[1]

Similarly, Irenaeus writing from Gaul c.170 declared:

> Luke...the companion of Paul, recorded in a book the gospel preached by him.[2]

Irenaeus describes how a heretic treated the Gospel of Luke in the early 140s:

> Marcion...mutilates the gospel which is according to Luke, removing all that is written respecting the

generation of the Lord, and sets aside a great deal of
the teaching of the teachings of the Lord...[2]

According to these authorities, the writer of the third
gospel was Luke, Paul's companion.

Second, those early writers were convinced that Luke
was not an eyewitness. One example will suffice—the
Muratorian Canon says:

Yet neither did he [Luke] see the Lord in the flesh; and
he too, as he was able to ascertain events, begins his
story from the birth of John.[1]

Luke's gospel begins this way:

Inasmuch as many have undertaken to compile a
narrative of the things which have been accomplished
among us, just as they were delivered to us by those
who from the beginning were eyewitnesses and
ministers of the word, it seemed good to me also...to
write an orderly account for you, most excellent
Theophilus, that you may know the truth concerning
the things of which you have been informed.

From this we infer the following:

1 Certain "eyewitnesses" had compiled "narratives"
about Jesus.

2 They "delivered" these to Luke, who was not an
eyewitness.

3 Using these, Luke has written up a more comprehensive history.

Who were these "eyewitnesses" and what were their
"narratives"? If Luke has woven together certain strands
as they were "delivered" to him, it may be possible for
us to tease them apart and examine them. This is the
science which is called Source Criticism. It tells us that
Luke used the following three strands:

1 Mark's gospel. Luke incorporates approximately
fifty per cent of Mark, which represents about
twenty-five per cent of Luke's total.

2 The Nativity stories (Chapters 1 and 2; about ten
per cent of Luke's total).

3 A document known as "Proto-Luke" (chapters

scattered through Luke but especially 9 to 18 and 22 to 24).

"Proto-Luke" was a document thought to be in existence earlier than Mark and composed of:

"Q"—A collection of sayings of Jesus referred to by scholars as "Q" (*Quelle* is German for source).

and

"L"—the source known as "L" is made up of

a) Narrative (e.g. Zacchaeus, trial before Herod)
b) Miracles (e.g. Healing of ten lepers)
c) Parables (e.g. Good Samaritan, Prodigal Son).

Let us leave for the moment the historical significance of these strands in Luke and the use he makes of them.

Matthew

Although the gospel according to Matthew was the most widely used, its origins are shrouded in mystery. The title of the gospel, which was in use by the middle of the second century, is intended to identify the author as Matthew, i.e. Levi the tax collector, one of the twelve disciples (Matthew 9:9 = Mark 2:14 = Luke 5:27). References to Matthew from the second century are not numerous.

Irenaeus c.170 wrote that:

Matthew also issued a written gospel among the Hebrews in their own dialect.[2]

Papias c.130 had commented:

Matthew compiled the oracles in the Hebrew language: but everyone interpreted them as he was able.[1]

As it is likely that Irenaeus merely echoes Papias, we probably have not two sources but one. Two things are clear from these references. First, the author was one of the twelve disciples. Second, he compiled, in Hebrew, the sayings of Jesus.

It is interesting to compare this early evidence about the gospel with the written gospel as we have it. The source critics have discovered three basic strands in Matthew:

1 Mark's gospel. Matthew reproduces ninety per cent of Mark's material, which represents about fifty per cent of Matthew's total.

2 The source known as "Q" which Luke also reproduces (as part of Proto-Luke), representing about twenty-five per cent of Matthew's total.

3 Material found only in Matthew, usually known as "M", representing about twenty-five per cent of Matthew's total.

Difficulties have been found with the comments about Matthew's gospel by Irenaeus and Papias. Why, for example, would an eyewitness need someone else's narrative (Mark's) when he could write his own? How can Papias claim Matthew "compiled oracles in the Hebrew language" when the gospel as we have it is written in Greek? What are the answers to these important questions?

One possible solution is that what Matthew originally wrote in Hebrew was the sayings source "Q", or perhaps the collection of Old Testament "proof texts" which form such a significant part of his gospel. In this case Matthew, or some other writer unknown to us, subsequently translated these "Hebrew oracles" into Greek and combined them with Mark and the other source(s), thus completing the gospel in its present form. But who the final author/editor was, and by what processes he gathered his sources, are matters about which there is no certain information.

What can be stated is that the gospel was in use at least by the nineties and that the author made use of the three sources: Mark, "Q" and "M".

Mark in Matthew and Luke

Luke and Matthew both incorporate pre-existent strands and weave them together into their respective gospels.

Earlier we saw that the other two evangelists, John and Mark, appear to be their own sources, John having been an eyewitness, Mark the companion of an eyewitness.

The use of earlier sources by Matthew and Luke has great significance for the question of the trustworthiness of these two writers. Of the four strands—Mark, "Q", "M", "L"—which Matthew and Luke use, Mark exists independently and "Q" is reproduced in both. We are immediately able to check the accuracy and the integrity of Matthew and Luke by their use of pre-existent sources, in particular Mark. What do we discover?

Let us investigate a particular case, part of the parable of the wicked tenants (see p.104):

Two comments may be made:

First, Matthew and Luke do not follow Mark slavishly. Both authors tell the story with fewer (Greek) words (Mark fifty, Luke forty-seven, Matthew forty-five) and with more polished expression. Hoskyns and Davey after an exhaustive comparison of Matthew's and Luke's use of Mark wrote:

> The authors of the two later gospels are concerned for their Greek readers. They add, in order to make clear what Jesus demands of his disciples. They simplify, in order to avoid crude misunderstanding. They omit what appears to be trivial and unnecessary. They order and arrange the tradition, in order that it may be the more easily read in public or in private, and they improve the grammar and style, in order that their intelligent readers may not be unreasonably provoked.[3]

Second, Jesus' statement about himself that he is the sender's (i.e. God's) "beloved son" is one of the most important theological statements in Mark. What do Matthew and Luke do with it? Luke reproduces it as it is, but Matthew actually omits "beloved", thus weakening the impact. Not that Matthew has a low view of Jesus: he is "Emmanuel, God with us" (1:23), the Son who alone knows the Father (11:27). Yet, so far from

Mark 12:5-7	Matthew 21:36-38	Luke 20:12-14
And he sent another, and him they killed; and so with many others, some they beat and some they killed.	Again he sent other servants, more than the first, and they did the same to them.	And he sent yet a third; this one they wounded and cast out.
He still had one other, a beloved son; finally he sent him to them saying, "They will respect my son".	Afterwards he sent his son to them, saying, "They will respect my son".	Then the owner of the vineyard said, "What shall I do? I will send my beloved son; it may be they will respect him".
But those tenants said to one another,	But when the tenants saw the son, they said to themselves,	But when the tenants saw him, they said to themselves,
"This is the heir; come, let us kill him and the inheritance will be ours."	"This is the heir; come, let us kill him and have his inheritance."	"This is the heir; let us kill him, that the inheritance may be ours."

expanding, elevating or magnifying the "Son" at this point, Matthew reduces him, for some reason. This example is typical of the way Luke and Matthew use Mark. Hoskyns and Davey commented:

But in the whole of this process of editing they nowhere heighten Mark's tremendous conception of Jesus. No deifying of a prophet or of a mere preacher of righteousness can be detected.[3]

When we make a close scrutiny of Matthew and Luke at work on the text of Mark we discover them to be careful scribes who do not exaggerate the claims of Jesus by the way they present them.

Luke's sober care may also be discerned in the account of the raising of the dead son of the widow of Nain, which is found only in Luke's gospel (7:11–17). The setting is one of profound tragedy. A woman who is without a husband has now lost her only son. She is left without visible means of support. Her family "line" is at an end. When Jesus saw the funeral procession near the city gate, he was moved with compassion and raised the boy to life again. Luke records the amazement of the onlookers and the sentiments they expressed. He could easily have had them say that "this was the Son of God" or "God was with them" or some other utterance to present an exalted view of Jesus. In fact Luke has not heightened the Christology as he might so easily have done as the one who also wrote the Acts of the Apostles, where the post-resurrection glory of Jesus is so important. Luke gives us instead the relatively mild verbal reaction of the onlookers. They said Jesus was a "great prophet"; and that is all.

Earlier sources as eyewitnesses

Since at the point where we can check them, namely in their work on Mark, Matthew and Luke they prove trustworthy, we are encouraged about their use of the other sources at their disposal.[4] "Q" is a substantial source which scholars study in its own right. It has its own distinctive structure, style and theological emphasis. Similarly, the contents and emphases of the other sources may also be scrutinized, though it is beyond the scope of this book to do so. What is clear from the first and third gospels is that the following sources were already in existence and by an early date:

Mark

Q

M

The Infancy Stories (Luke)

Proto-Luke (Q + L).

These sources emanate from either individuals or churches and as such they represent further independent evidence for Jesus. Luke states that the information which he has incorporated in his work has been handed over to him by *eyewitnesses* (1:2). Thus to John and Mark as primary sources for the story of Jesus we may also add Proto-Luke and/or "Q".

The style of Luke and Matthew

Although Matthew and Luke both make use of the gospel of Mark as well as "Q", their gospels are stylistically distinctive and aimed at different sets of readers. Neither gospel is a simple variation of the other. The author of the gospel of Matthew was a Jew who wrote for Jewish readers. Matthew did not need to explain, for example, what a phylactery[5] was—his Jewish audience already knew. Greater knowledge of the Jewish Talmud by Christian scholars has shown that in his presentation of the genealogy of Christ, his method of quoting the Old Testament, as well as his way of telling the stories about Jesus, Matthew is thoroughly Semitic. Matthew wrote about Christ from and for the Jewish culture of his time.

Luke, on the other hand, wrote for readers who were, like himself, educated and cultured Gentiles. Compare, for example, the prologue of Luke's second volume with the second volume of one of Josephus' works:

Acts 1:1	Against Apion ii, 1
In my former book, Theophilus, I wrote about all that Jesus began to do and to teach...	In the first volume of my work, my most esteemed Epaphroditus, I demonstrated the antiquity of our race...

The similarities are striking. Both authors refer back to an earlier volume, briefly stating its contents; both dedicate their books to individuals whom they mention by name. Details such as these were literary conventions in vogue among educated Gentiles which Luke and Josephus both observed.

Clearly, then, Matthew and Luke belonged to separate cultural groups and to which, respectively, they addressed their gospels. In assessing the competence of Matthew or Luke as historians it would be unfair to compare them either with modern biographers or with one another. If comparison is to be made, it must be with other writers from the cultural group to which each belonged.

The character of the source strands

Are these source strands historical in character? We would possibly expect them not to be, since they consist mostly of isolated teachings of Jesus with only the "L" source supplying any significant narrative information. It is interesting to compare these synoptic source strands in their original form with the Mishnah, a collection of the sayings of the rabbis written more than a century after the gospels. These sayings of the rabbis, which relate to legal and ethical matters within Judaism, contain virtually no details embedded within them which might indicate where or when or under what circumstances they were originally uttered. The source strands of the synoptic gospels, on the other hand, do contain some historical specifics, which are, however, mostly related to geographic details. Let us consider some examples.

The "Q" source

The "Q" source mentions that, after his baptism "Jesus returned from the Jordan" (Luke 4:1 = Matthew 4:1) and that later he "entered into Capernaum" (Luke 7:1 = Matthew 8:5).

In a famous teaching passage, Jesus pronounced woes upon the northern cities of Chorazin, Bethsaida and Capernaum (Luke 10:13-15 = Matthew 11:21-23) which the twelve visited during their mission.

The "M" source

The geographic references in "M" are but few, being confined to Capernaum (Matthew 17:24), Jerusalem (21:10) and "Galilee...a mountain" (28:16). Jesus instructed his disciples not to visit Gentile areas or any city of the Samaritans (10:5).

The "L" source

The relatively greater historical interest of Luke is evident in the "L" source, which in all probability he compiled. He stated that the ministry of John the Baptist commenced in the "fifteenth year of...Tiberius Caesar [AD 28 or 29], Pontius Pilate being governor of Judaea, and Herod [Antipas] being tetrarch of Galilee and his brother Philip tetrarch of the region of Ituraea and Trachonitis and Lysanias tetrarch of Abilene, in the high priesthood of Annas and Caiaphas" (Luke 3:1-2).

This detailed statement, which mentions the Roman Emperor and his local governor as well as the Jewish tetrarchs and high priests, is corroborated as accurate by external sources. In addition, "L" refers to such places as Nazareth (Luke 4:16), the lake of Gennesaret (5:1), a city called Nain (7:11), "passing between Samaria and Galilee" (17:11), Jericho (19:1), Jerusalem (19:11), the

Mount of Olives (19:37) and a village named Emmaus (24:13).

The "L" strand also mentions a number of people by name, for example: Mary Magdalene. . .Joanna, the wife of Chuza, Herod's steward, and Susanna (Luke 8:2–3), Martha and Mary (10:38–39), Zacchaeus. . .a chief tax collector (19:2) and Cleopas (24:18).

While the source strands vary between the relative naiveté of "M" to the historical sophistication of "L", their historical character is evident, especially when one bears in mind the sayings of the Mishnah for which there is an almost total lack of historical "landmarks".

Two things can be said with confidence about Matthew and Luke. First, as we check their use of Mark we find that Matthew and Luke are responsible scribes who do not exaggerate the material at their disposal. Second, we discover, hidden within their gospels, strands which existed before Matthew and Luke wrote, as sources of information about Jesus. The evidence for what Jesus did and said is significantly more extensive and complex than we might suspect from the four gospels as they stand.

Further reading to Chapter Eight:

W. Barclay, *The Gospels and Acts* vol.1, S.C.M., London, 1976.

E.C. Hoskyns and N. Davey, *The Riddle of the New Testament*, Faber, London, no date.

I.H. Marshall (Ed), *New Testament Interpretation*, Paternoster, Exeter, 1977.

R.P. Martin, *New Testament Foundations* vol.1, Eerdmans, Grand Rapids, 1975.

Notes
[1]Quoted in J. STEVENSON, *a New Eusebuis*, S.P.C.K., 1957

[2]*Against Heresies*, Ante-Nicene Fathers, 3.1.1.

[3]*The Riddle of the New Testament*, Faber, London, no date, p.103.

[4]It is probable, but not certain, that these were written sources. *See* A.M. Hunter, *The Work and Words of Jesus*, London, 1958 where the sources "Q", "M", "L" are reproduced separately.

[5]A box containing Scripture verses. Worn on forehead and arms. See Matthew 23:5.

CHAPTER NINE

Miracles and the Modern World

Your reaction to the title of this chapter may be to say, "Modern man cannot be expected to believe that Jesus performed miracles". You may say, "People today know that the world is governed by the laws of nature, therefore miracles, or variations in those laws, simply cannot happen". "Since we don't see miracles nowadays," you may add, "the miracles in the New Testament must have arisen from the superstitious imagination of a pre-scientific age. Perhaps people at that time *thought* a miracle had taken place or *hoped* it had, but really they were mistaken."

The theologian will reply that it is Jesus, the central figure of the New Testament, who makes the difference. It is because God chose to "visit" our world at that time and place, in the person of his son, that extraordinary things happened in relationship to him. Understand that the great miracle is the incarnation of the Son of God, they argue, and the miracles are reasonable to believe. Indeed, if Jesus was "Emmanuel...God with us" (Matthew 1:23) we should be surprised if miracles did not take place.

When we turn to the gospels we find that the miracles of Jesus are pointed to as evidence of his true identity. Let us examine three sayings of Jesus which make this point.

The first is from the source known as "Q", from which Matthew and Luke both quote:

If it is by the Spirit ["'finger'', Luke] of God that I cast
out demons then the kingdom of God has come upon
you. (Matthew 12:28 = Luke 11:20)

Jesus was the bearer of the kingdom or rule of God
among them. In Jesus, God's will was being done on
earth; God's kingdom had come. The miraculous exor-
cisms pointed to the presence of the kingdom in Jesus.

The second example is found in a passage in the gospel
of Mark where Jesus provocatively declares a paralysed
man's sins forgiven. When challenged that only God
could forgive sins, Jesus declared:

But that you may know that the Son of Man has
authority on earth to forgive sins... I say to you, rise,
take up your pallet [bed] and go home. (Mark 2:10,11)

The miraculous healing of the man served to establish
the shattering truth that Jesus, the Son of Man, bore the
authority of God among men to forgive sins.

The third example is taken from the gospel of John:

If I am not doing the works of my Father, then do not
believe me; but if I do them, even though you do not
believe me, believe the works, that you may know and
understand that the Father is in me and I am in the
Father. (10:37–38 cf. 14:10–11)

If his hearers doubt what he says about himself, then let
them look at what he does—what he calls ''works of my
Father''. The miracle works of Jesus in giving sight to the
blind and life to the dead are the works of God his Father,
full of compassion and divine power.

Jesus' contemporaries sensed that he possessed super-
natural powers. There is good evidence (Mark 8:11;
Matthew 12:38,39) that they requested him to perform a
heavenly sign, that is, to do something freakish or
abnormal. Jesus' miracles of healing the sick or feeding
the hungry (see John 6:30) were too mundane or ordinary
to satisfy their craving for spectacular evidence.

Unquestionably, the miracles of Jesus were restrained,
always done for the good of those in need and not for
show. Nevertheless, the effect of such actions was to

indicate that the kingdom of God had come among them, that the Son of Man was present with them, authorised to forgive sins, and that the "Father was in him".

But are the miracles historical? Can modern man be given reasonable evidence for him to believe they took place? There are four reasons for confidence in the historicity of the miracles of Jesus.

First, there is evidence from the non-Christian sources, Josephus and the Talmud. Josephus, writing in the nineties, clearly intends us to understand that Jesus performed miracles when he states that "Jesus... wrought surprising feats".[1] The Talmud, written much later, says that "They hanged Yeshu" because "he practised sorcery"[2] which is probably a reference to exorcism by the power of the devil, something Jesus was accused of in the gospel account (Mark 3:22).

Second, the apostle Peter refers to the miracles of Jesus in his two major speeches as recorded in the Acts of the Apostles. On the day of Pentecost in the year 33 in Jerusalem Peter said:

Jesus of Nazareth, a man attested to you by God with mighty works and wonders and signs which God did through him in your midst, as you yourselves know. (Acts 2:22)

Four or five years later, at the house of the centurion Cornelius in Caesarea Peter stated that:

God anointed Jesus of Nazareth with the Holy Spirit and with power; how he went about doing good and healing all who were oppressed by the devil. (Acts 10:38)

Like the crowds in Jerusalem, Cornelius also knew of these remarkable deeds of Jesus (Acts 10:37). The Acts' speeches of Peter and Paul contain important historical information about Jesus. Paul makes no reference to Jesus' miracles, an omission that actually encourages our confidence in the authenticity of the speeches, since Paul was not an eyewitness to the historical Jesus.

Third, some scholars find the sayings of Jesus about

miracles particularly significant, specially those which are readily translatable back into Aramaic, the language he spoke. Consider, for example, Jesus' reply to the messengers from John the Baptist:

Tell John what you hear and see: the blind receive their sight and the lame walk, lepers are cleansed and the deaf hear, and the dead are raised up (Matthew 11:4,5).

J. Jeremias, an expert in Aramaic, argued that these words originally occurred in a speech rhythm which was characteristic of the way Jesus spoke.[3] In what is unquestionably an utterance of Jesus, appeal is made to what has been seen and heard in respect to miracles of healing the blind, the lame, the lepers, the deaf, and raising the dead.

Again, in a passage common to Matthew and Luke, that is, belonging to the sayings source "Q", Jesus said:

Woe unto thee, Chorazin, woe unto thee, Bethsaida, for if the mighty works which were done in you had been done in Tyre and Sidon, they would have repented long ago...And thou Capernaum... (Matthew 11:21,23; Luke 10:13–15).

Once more in a saying which is undoubtedly historical, Jesus appeals to miraculous events which, by common agreement, had happened in Chorazin, Bethsaida and Capernaum. This is powerful evidence for the historical truth of the miracles as Jeremias, who subjects the Scriptures to rigorous criticism, himself commented:

Thus even when strict critical standards have been applied to the miracle stories, a demonstrably historical nucleus remains. Jesus performed healings which astonished his contemporaries.[4]

Fourth, there are many examples of multiple attestation to exorcism, nature miracles, healings and the raising of the dead in the primary gospel sources Mark, John, "Q", "L", and "M", as the following clearly shows:[5]

	Mark	John	"Q"	"L"	"M"
Exorcism	Capernaum demoniac (1:21–28) Gerasene demoniac (5:1–20)				The dumb demoniac (9:32–34) cf 10:5–8)
Nature Miracles	Stilling the storm (4:35–41) Feeding the five thousand (6:30–44) Walking on the water (6:45–52)	Feeding the five thousand (6:1–13) Walking on the water (6:16–21)		Draft of fishes (5:1–11)	
Healing	Withered hand (3:1–6) Blind Bartimaeus (10:46–52)	Official's son (4:46–54) Man born blind (9:1–34)	Centurion's boy (Matthew 8:5–13)	Bent woman (13:10–17)	
Resurrection	Daughter of Jairus (5:21–43)	Lazarus (11:1–44)		Widow's son (7:11–17)	

It is important to note that the sources cited here arose independently of each other. Notice too that the whole range of miracle actions is attested. The breadth of attestation of the whole gamut of the miracles of Jesus is very compelling historical evidence. Nature miracles, for example, are described in four of these five independent sources.

The evidence from non-Christian sources, from the Acts speeches, from the sayings of Jesus, and from the primary gospel strands combine to provide a solid basis for historical confidence in the miracles of Jesus. One might even say that this evidence is as good as, or better than, that for most other historical events or persons of that period.

Further reading to Chapter Nine:

R.T. France, *The Man They Crucified*, I.V.P., London, 1975.

R.H. Fuller, *Interpreting the Miracles*, S.C.M., London, 1963.

J. Jeremias, *New Testament Theology* I, S.C.M., London, 1971.

C.S. Lewis, *Miracles*, Fontana, Glasgow, 1978.

B. Meyer, *The Aims of Jesus*, S.C.M., London, 1979.

H.E.W. Turner, *Jesus, Master and Lord*, Mowbray, London, 1957.

G. Vermes, *Jesus the Jew*, Collins, London, 1973.

Notes
[1]*Antiquities* 18:63.

[2]*Sanhedrin* 43a.

[3]*New Testament Theology* I, S.C.M., London, 1971, p.21.

[4]*Op. cit.*, p.92.

[5]For an exhaustive list of miracles see R.H. Fuller, *Interpreting the Miracles*, S.C.M., London, 1963, pp.126–127.

CHAPTER TEN

The Birth of Jesus

Our two eyewitness sources, John and Mark, say nothing about the birth and boyhood of Jesus, although they refer to his mother and siblings (Mark 6:3; cf. 3:31; John 6:42, 7:3,5,10). It is only as an adult at the threshold of his ministry that John and Mark introduce Jesus to their readers.

The New Testament letters, including Paul's, are silent about the details of Jesus' birth and upbringing.

Our only information comes from Matthew and Luke. But is it trustworthy? What if these authors have contrived the birth stories as an introduction to an otherwise already completed story? Maybe the nativity stories are pious fiction and nothing more? This is certainly what some people think.

Perhaps church people have themselves fostered the idea—no doubt unintentionally. It sometimes seems that aesthetics rather than truth predominate in the Christian celebrations of Christmas. The rich tradition of Christmas music, combined with the sentiment of the occasion, often all but obliterate the question of historical reality. If baby Jesus has been reduced in the minds of many to the same level of mythological unreality as Santa Claus, do the Christians have anyone but themselves to blame?

Let me give two reasons for confidence in the truth of the stories which deal with the birth of Jesus.

The agreement of Matthew and Luke

There can be no doubt that Matthew and Luke wrote independently of each other. Matthew, as he wrote his scroll, did not have Luke's before him, nor did Luke have Matthew's. The difference of style and content make that clear. There can be no suggestion of copying or dependence of the one upon the other.

Yet these authors innocently agree at a number of critical points. In both gospels Jesus is born in *Bethlehem*. This, apparently, is not a detail which was widely known. On one occasion recorded by John, the crowd specifically rejected Jesus as Messiah because he was a Galilean. "Messiah...comes from Bethlehem," they said (John 7:42), accurately quoting the ancient prophet (Micah 5:2). The manner in which John recounts the incident shows that he knew, even if others did not, that Jesus was born in Bethlehem.

Both Matthew and Luke indicate that Joseph, the legal father, is a *descendant* of King *David* (Matthew 1:16; Luke 1:27,32). Though Mark makes no mention of Joseph, John twice refers to Jesus as "son of Joseph" (1:45; 6:42). Nevertheless, Mark clearly teaches that Jesus is the "son of David" (Mark 10:47,48; 11:10; 12:35–37), something that John also knows, but makes nothing of (John 7:42).

In both Matthew and Luke, Mary the mother of Jesus was a *virgin* when she conceived him (Matthew 1:18; Luke 1:35). In quite a subtle way John also appears to betray a knowledge of the virgin birth in his reference to the Christians' spiritual *re*birth.

> ...children of God; who were born, not of blood nor of the will of the flesh nor of the will of man, but of God (John 1:12,13).

These words also describe the manner of the conception of Jesus of Nazareth, which occurred independently of "blood", "the will of the flesh" or "the will of man" but which depended directly upon God.

Matthew and Luke also agree as to when Jesus was

born. *It was during the time* (37 BC to 4 BC) *when Herod the Great was king of Israel* (Matthew 2:1; Luke 1:5, 24–26).

These impressive points of agreement, which are clearly uncontrived, are the more compelling when we consider the difference of perspective and emphasis in the two accounts. For his part, Luke shows the reader that Elizabeth, mother of John the Baptist, and Mary were cousins. He tells us that the angel's name was Gabriel. Matthew mentions neither of these details. Luke states that it was for some kind of registration or census that Joseph and Mary came from Nazareth to Bethlehem. Matthew, by contrast, implies that Joseph and Mary only returned to settle in Nazareth in Galilee after their escape to, and refuge in, Egypt (2:22). Matthew refers to the visit of the wise men, the jealousy of Herod, the slaughter of the children, the flight into Egypt, and tells of the resettlement of Galilee because of Archelaus who had succeeded his father Herod in Judaea. Luke is silent on these details.

The differences in the narratives indicate that not only were Matthew and Luke isolated from each other when they wrote, but also that the sources on which they depended were quite separate. Yet from these underlying independent source strands, we have detailed agreement about where Jesus was born, when, to which parents and the miraculous circumstances of his conception.

It may be agreed that, in the form in which the stories are told, Luke in particular has been influenced by certain narratives from the Old Testament. The account of the conception of John the Baptist is similar to the account of the conception of Samson (Luke 1:5–7 cf. Judges 13:2–5), while Mary's song of praise resembles Hannah's song (Luke 1:46–55, cf. 1 Samuel 2:1–10). This means only that Luke has consciously modelled his style, and Mary her song, on certain parts of the Old Testament in order to show their belief that the same God was active in their affairs, as he was in former times. The facts about which Matthew and Luke agree, both innocently and independently, leave little doubt that we are dealing with history and reality and not pious fiction.

The stories are consistent with known history

Some years ago, when researching the broad stream of Jewish history during the times of Herod the Great, I was struck by the way several aspects of the birth stories fitted in. Fortunately we have as a source the Jewish historian Josephus, whose description of the last years of Herod is extensive. A good way to get a "feel" for the period is to read relevant sections of his *Jewish War* and *Jewish Antiquities*.

Since Herod died in 4 BC, Jesus must have been born in 7 or 6 BC to satisfy the detail of the search for boys two years old (Matthew 2:16). Thus when the year 2000 comes it will really be 2006 or 2007! Why is our Anno Domini calendar incorrect? Simply because the sixth century monk Dionysius, when reforming the Roman calender along Christian lines to pivot around the birth of Jesus, miscalculated the date of the death of Herod relative to the founding of Rome, the previous starting point for western calendars.

Augustus instituted the practice of levying taxes from "all the world" (Luke 2:1), by which Luke means all the people within the Roman Empire. To prevent tax evasion, all members of the provinces were registered or enrolled, a process which in Gaul, for example, took forty years to complete. We know of registrations in Egypt which were commenced in 10 BC and repeated every fourteen years. But this does not mean that registrations everywhere occurred at that time. Some provinces had been incorporated into the empire only recently and were not yet ready for this procedure. A problem in Luke's account is that according to Luke 1:5 (and Matthew 1-2), Jesus was born during the reign of Herod (37–4 BC), which was before Quirinius became governor of Syria (AD 6–9), and in whose time the registration is said to have occurred (Luke 2:1). Herod died ten years before Quirinius' registration, during which Luke appears to say Jesus was born (Luke 2:2-7).

Lack of evidence makes it difficult to be certain, but Luke could be referring to a lengthy process of registration which may have begun during Herod's reign (perhaps at the time of the taking of the oath of allegiance to Herod and Augustus 7 BC?) and which was summarily concluded after AD 6 when Judaea was formally annexed to Rome at the time of Quirinius' appointment as Governor of Syria. Quirinius was a very senior Roman official who had served previously in provinces adjacent to Syria. The registrations of Jews may have begun while Quirinius held a roving command in the East prior to his formal appointment to Syria. Whatever the precise details, Luke's account of Joseph and Mary undergoing registration, for taxation and possibly also for an oath of loyalty, is thoroughly consistent with the established practice within the empire.

The "wise men [Greek: *magoi*] from the east" (Matthew 2:1) are able to be identified with astrologers from Mesopotamia, the ancient home of the science-cum-superstitition of "star gazing". A large community of Jews also lived there.

One of the great prophecies of the Old Testament, which would affect not only the Jews, but the whole world, concerned a star. According to Numbers 24:17,

> ...star shall come forth out of Jacob, and a sceptre shall rise out of Israel.

Centuries before Christ, the Jews interpreted this to mean that from the Jewish people would arise a ruler of the whole world. The Greek translation of the Old Testament for example, translates Numbers 24:17 as,

> a star shall come forth out of Jacob, a man shall arise...

A hundred years after Christ, Rabbi Akiba saw ben Kosiba as that star who would rule the world. Akiba renamed him bar Kokhba, "son of a star". The Gentiles also knew of this Jewish prophecy. Both Tacitus and Suetonius refer to it. Tacitus, for example, writes of "a mysterious prophecy...of the ancient scriptures of their priests" whereby,

the Orient would triumph and from Judaea would go forth men destined to rule the world.[1]

Tacitus changed the prophecy from the singular "man" to the plural "men", seeing the fulfilment in father and son Vespasian and Titus who, as the Roman victors of the Jews AD 66-70, were both destined to become Emperors. It is probable that a version of this prophecy was known by the *magoi* from Mesopotamia.

Every 805 years the planets Jupiter and Saturn draw near to each other. Astronomers have calculated that in 7 BC the two planets were conjoined three times—in May, September and December and that in February, 6 BC they were joined by Mars, presenting a spectacular triangular conjunction.[2] It appears likely that the *magoi*, knowing the ancient star prophecy, on seeing the brilliant planetary formation, decided to visit Judaea to see the new king of the world. Incidentally, the Biblical record does not say there were three *magoi*.

In 1871 the astronomer John Williams published his authoritative list of sightings of Comets. Comet number 52 on Williams' list appeared for seventy days early in 5 BC and would have been visible in the Middle East. Was this the "star" which guided the *magoi*? Why did Herod kill the boys who were two years old and younger? Could this figure be explained by the time in 7-6 BC when the conjunction of the stars appeared?

Time Magazine, in its cover story of 27 December 1976, commented that while "there are those who dismiss the star as nothing more than a metaphor...others take the Christmas star more literally, and not without reason. Astronomical records show that there were several significant celestial events around the time of Jesus' birth".

Herod's paranoia in ordering the killing of the baby

boys of Bethlehem is entirely in character. Earlier in his
reign the king had murdered his wife Mariamne. More
recently, he had removed two sons, prompting Augustus'
grim joke that it was safer to be Herod's pig than Herod's
son. The king was scrupulous not to break the Old Testament ban on eating pig meat but he cared little about the
sixth commandment. Later, knowing his own death was
close, Herod ordered the arrest of the distinguished men
from every village of Judaea. They were herded together
in the Hippodrome in Jerusalem. Herod ordered,

> "The moment I expire have them...massacred; so
> shall all Judaea and every household weep for me,
> whether they will or no..."[3]

The order was not carried out. But the incident shows
that the one who was capable of issuing it was also
capable of "the slaughter of the innocents".

There is a possible reference to the slaughter of the
baby boys in the fourth century AD pagan writer
Macrobius who describes the reaction of the Emperor
Augustus to news from Palestine which had recently
come to him:

> When he [Augustus] heard that Herod king of the Jews
> had ordered all the boys in Syria under the age of two
> years to be put to death and that the king's son was
> among those killed, he said, "I'd rather be Herod's
> pig [hus] than Herod's son [huios]".[4]

Unfortunately we don't know Macrobius' source or
sources of information. It appears that he has fused into
one episode two separate events—namely the killing of
the baby boys and Herod's murder of a son of his own,
who was then an adult and removed in circumstances
different from those of the children. It does not seem that
Macrobius merely quotes Matthew's story, since he was
a convinced pagan and the reference to Syria is at odds
with Matthew's version. It is more likely that the killing
of the boys was recorded in a pagan source, now lost to
us, but preserved in Macrobius. This extract may

provide striking confirmation of Matthew's account that Herod the Great ordered the killing of male children two years and younger.

Are the stories about the birth of Jesus historically reliable? Enough has been written, I believe, to indicate it to be perfectly reasonable to accept their historicity. Matthew and Luke, though clearly independent of each other, agree on the major details of when and where it occurred, as well as the miraculous conception of the child. Moreover, many incidental details in the stories fit unobtrusively yet consistently into the known background of Jewish history. But a word of caution. See Christ as he was through the sober lenses of the gospels, not through the rose-coloured spectacles of popular Christmas tradition.

Further reading to Chapter Ten:
P.L. Maier, *First Christmas*, Mowbrays, London, 1971.
R.T. France, "Scripture, Tradition and History in the Infancy Narratives of Matthew", in *Gospel Perspectives II*, R.T. France and D. Wenham (eds), J.S.O.T. Press, Sheffield, 1981.

Notes
[1]*Histories*, 5:13.

[2]*Time* Magazine, 27 December 1976, p.27.

[3]Josephus, *Jewish War* I, 660.

[4]Macrobius, *The Saturnalia*, Tr. P.V. Davis, Columbia University Press, New York, 1969, p.171.

CHAPTER ELEVEN

Paul and the Historical Jesus

Paul wrote his letters within the period AD 50–65(?).[1] So far as we know, the written gospels were not in existence when he began writing. What can we learn from Paul about the historical Jesus? How much would we know about Jesus if the gospels did not exist and we were solely dependent upon Paul?

Revelation and tradition

Paul's knowledge of Jesus can be summed up in two Greek works *apokalupsis* and *paradosis*. The first word is related to the verb "to veil" (*kaluptein*). When *apo* is prefixed it means "*un*veil" or "reveal". Thus the noun *apokalupsis* signifies "unveiling" or "revelation". Paul wrote to the Galatians that,

the gospel which was preached by me is not man's gospel...it came through a *revelation* of Jesus Christ (Galatians 1:11,12).

It was on the road near Damascus that God "...was pleased to reveal his Son" to (him) (Galatians 1:16). Paul's life as a Christian and also as an apostle began at the moment of that remarkable event. Moreover, what God revealed to Paul in Christ in that instant became the framework of Paul's thinking about Christ. Henceforth, Paul would speak about Jesus as "the Son of God"

(Galatians 1:16; Acts 9:20; cf. 1 Thessalonians 1:10; 2 Corinthians 1:19; Romans 1:4); as the "highly exalted...Lord" (Acts 9:5; 22:10; 26:15; Philippians 2:9,11; 2 Corinthians 4:5); as "the image of God" (2 Corinthians 3:18; 4:4); as "glorious" (Acts 22:11; 9:3; 22:6; 2 Corinthians 4:4,6); and as "the man of heaven" (1 Corinthians 15:49).

To say that the Damascus Road event radically changed the direction of Paul's life is to tell only part of the story; his view of who Christ was, entered into and became a permanent part of his thinking at that point. While for Paul the focus of interest was always the heavenly Lord, he knew certain things about the historical Lord. It is those historical details which concern us in this chapter.

We turn therefore to the second word, *paradosis*, "tradition". *Paradosis* means "a handing over" as of a prisoner from one gaoler to another or of a piece of information from a teacher to a pupil. It was used in this latter sense of a lesson or teaching which a rabbi would impart to his disciple. Thus, the rabbis handed over their teachings intact, generation by generation, to their pupils, who would in turn become rabbis. The usual English translation "traditions", a word which is often taken to mean "old things", fails to capture the dynamic "handing over" idea which is intrinsic to *paradosis*.

The traditions: from whom did Paul receive them?

In the course of time Paul would, rabbi-like, hand over important pieces of information (*paradoseis*) about Jesus to the churches. First, however, he must receive them from those who were Christian teachers before him. In writing to the Corinthians Paul mentions both the "receiving" and the "delivering" of the *paradosis* about the gospel:

I delivered to you...what I also received (1 Corinthians 15:3).

Earlier in this letter he repeated what he "delivered" to

the Corinthians about the Last Supper, having previously "received" it from the Lord.

> I received from the Lord what I also delivered to you, that the Lord Jesus on the night when he was betrayed took bread..." (1 Corinthians 11:23).

This passage is striking. It refers both to the heavenly Lord ("the Lord") from whom Paul received the *paradosis* and also the historical Lord ("the Lord Jesus"). The heavenly Lord is seen as the one from whom Paul received the *paradosis*, even though it originated in history with the historical Lord "Who on the night he was betrayed took bread..."

What Paul omits to tell us is through whom he received that *paradosis*. I assume it to be the same person(s) from whom Paul received the *paradosis* about the gospel, mentioned above. When did Paul receive these *paradoseis* and from whom?

Paul's first contact as a Christian with other Christians was in Damascus immediately following his momentous encounter with Christ on the way there (Acts 9 and 22). Ananias told Paul to "...be baptized and wash away your sins, calling on his name" (Acts 22:16).

Paul was thrust straightaway into a new world in which he must learn about baptism, forgiveness, the name of Jesus (his deity), faith and doubtless many other things as well. Was it in Damascus that Paul received the *paradoseis* about the gospel and the Lord's Supper?

Jerusalem is, I believe, more likely. It was to Jerusalem that Paul went within three years of his conversion:

> to visit Cephas, and [I] remained with him fifteen days. But I saw none of the other apostles except James the Lord's brother (Galatians 1:18–19).

Cephas (= Peter) and James, the only two persons Paul visited in Jerusalem, are the two apostles named elsewhere in the list of people who saw the risen Christ (1 Corinthians 15:5–7).[2] What is significant is that this list of witnesses is part of the *paradosis* about the gospel which Paul "received". There can be little doubt, therefore, that Paul received this *paradosis* and also the one relating to the Lord's Supper at Jerusalem c.36 from Peter (and James?).

Peter, Paul and James with the others mentioned hold in common the one *paradosis*, namely:

that Christ died for our sins in accordance with the scriptures, that he was buried, that he was raised on the third day in accordance with the scriptures...that he appeared to Cephas...to the twelve...to more than five hundred...to James...to all the apostles...to *me* (1 Corinthians 15:3–8).

Paul concludes:

whether then it was I or *they* [in particular *Peter* and *James*]

so *we* preach [in particular *Peter, James* and *Paul*]

and so *you* [Corinthians] believed (1 Corinthians 15:11).

From whom then did Paul receive information about the historical Jesus? So far as we can see, Paul himself had neither seen nor heard Jesus of Nazareth. Nevertheless he was converted soon after the resurrection, perhaps within eighteen months.[3] Therefore his contact with Christians in Damascus (Acts 9:19) was very close in time to Jesus of Nazareth. Paul was an early convert to Christianity.

Within three years of his conversion (Galatians 1:18 = Acts 9:26), he came to Jerusalem where he "visited" Peter and "saw" James from whom, it appears, he "received" the *paradoseis* about the Lord's Supper and the gospel. This is not to suggest that the stories and sayings of Jesus had all been systematically collected by the time of Paul's first visit to Jerusalem.

His second visit was made fourteen years after his conversion (Galatians 2:1 = Acts 21:17), that is in c.47. It is reasonable to assume that some of the sources referred to by Luke (1:2) and detectable within Luke's and Matthew's gospels were finalized by that time. It may also be assumed that Paul came to be aware of these

sources on this and subsequent visits to Jerusalem (c.49—
Acts 15:4; c.52—18:22).

If one bridge from Paul to the historical Jesus was his
contact with the Jerusalem church through visits in c.36,
47, 49, and 52, another was his association outside Jerusalem with the witness and apostle Peter (Galatians 2:11)
and with Barnabas, whose membership in the Jerusalem
church went back to the earliest times (Acts 4:36,37).
Barnabas was in daily contact with Paul for four or five
years (Acts 11:25,30; 12:25; 13:1,2 to 14:28; 15:2,4,12,
36-39). Barnabas, whose conversion was closer in time to
Christ than Paul's and who had been for a decade and a
half in the fellowship of the original companions of Jesus,
must have talked often to Paul about the historical Lord.

In sum, Paul had many opportunities to receive the
paradoseis of the Jerusalem church and to learn about the
life and teachings of Jesus of Nazareth.

It has been shown that the close correlation between
certain well-defined sections in Paul's writings, for
example Romans 12-14, with the reports of the teaching
of Jesus, from the common source which lies behind Luke
6:27-38 and Matthew 5:38-48, is evidence that Paul had
access to such teachings and passed them on to the
Gentile churches.[4] Paul's prayer to God as "Abba"
(Romans 8:15; Galatians 4:6) clearly derives from Jesus
(e.g. Mark 14:36), as does a probable reference to the
Lord's Prayer in the expression "Forbearing one another
and...forgiving each other" (Colossians 3:13). Some
scholars believe that Paul refers to the rural imagery of
Jesus, as well as to the parables.[5]

The historical Jesus: his birth and death

Birth and death are fundamental to human experience. A
modern biographer is interested in the details surrounding the birth and death of his chief character. While only
two evangelists describe the birth of Jesus, all four enter
into great detail about his death. The apostle Paul,

however, supplies no historical details about either the birth or the death of Jesus.

What Paul dwells on is the fact and the meaning of the birth and the death of Jesus, which are all of a piece in this famous sentence:

> For you know the grace of our Lord Jesus Christ, that though he was rich, yet for your sake he became poor, so that by his poverty you might become rich (2 Corinthians 8:9).

Here we see the fact of his incarnation and death, ("he became poor") and its meaning ("the grace of our Lord Jesus Christ"), but no historical details are given.

In Paul's thought the coming of Jesus into the world was necessary so that he might die. Thus:

> When the time had fully come, God sent forth his Son, born of [a] woman, born under the law, to redeem... (Galatians 4:4,5).

Paul knew that Jesus was brought up as a strict Jew ("born under the law"). The absence of reference to Jesus' father may mean that Paul knew of the virgin birth of Christ.

The fact and meaning of the death of the historical Lord are set out powerfully in the statement:

> For our sake [God] made him to be sin who knew no sin, so that in him we might become the righteousness of God (2 Corinthians 5:21).

Notice that although no historical details are supplied in these statements about Jesus' birth and death, they appear to be known by the writer.

Thus, "he became poor" (2 Corinthians 8:9) is entirely consistent with the details in the nativity stories of Matthew and Luke. The general comment "born of a woman" implies that the writer knew specifically which woman. In relation to the death of Jesus, the apostle often refers to crucifixion as the mode of execution (Galatians 3:1) and many have seen in the words "[God] made [Jesus] to be sin" an allusion to Jesus' cry of dereliction from the cross (Mark 15:34). The way Paul speaks of the fact and the meaning of the birth and death of Jesus implies some knowledge of historical details, which however, he does not supply.

The historical Jesus: his life
Paul gives only a few details from the life of Jesus:

1 He descended from Abraham (Galatians 3:16).

2 He was a Son of David (Romans 1:3).

3 He was naturally born but [perhaps?] supernaturally conceived (Galatians 4:4).

4 He was born and lived under the Jewish Law (Galatians 4:4).

5 He welcomed people (Romans 15:5,7).

6 His lifestyle was one of humility and service (Philippians 2:7,8).

7 He was abused and insulted during his life (Romans 15:3).

8 He had a brother named James (Galatians 1:19) and other unnamed brothers (1 Corinthians 9:5).

9 His disciple Peter was married (1 Corinthians 9:5; cf. Mark 1:30).

10 He instituted a memorial meal on the night of his betrayal (1 Corinthians 11:23–25).

11 He was betrayed (1 Corinthians 11:23).

12 He gave testimony before Pontius Pilate (1 Timothy 6:13).

13 He was killed by Jews of Judaea (1 Thessalonians 2:14,15).

14 He was buried, rose the third day and was thereafter seen alive on a number of occasions by many witnesses (1 Corinthians 15:4–8).

Although the information is limited it is noteworthy in two ways.

First, the details are conveyed incidentally and innocently. It seems that, if another theological point were to be made, the author was capable of introducing further historical facts. The implication is that Paul the apostle knew more about the historical Jesus than he says; presumably he saw no need to give further information.

Second, every detail given by Paul is, without exception, confirmed by the gospel narratives. His statements are free of exaggeration or distortion. This is all the more impressive because Paul's chief focus was not the historical, but the heavenly, Lord.

The historical Jesus: his teachings

The apostle Paul reproduces relatively few of the teachings of Jesus:

1	The Lord's Supper	1 Corinthians 11:23-25; cf. Mark 14:22-25.
2	Divorce and remarriage	1 Corinthians 7:10,11; cf. Mark 10:1-12.
3	The labourer deserves wages	1 Corinthians 9:14; cf. Matthew 10:10; Luke 10:7.
4	Eat what is set before you	1 Corinthians 10:27; cf. Luke 10:7.
5	Tribute to whom due	Romans 13:7; cf. Mark 12:13-17.
6	Thief in the night	1 Thessalonians 5:2-5 cf. Luke 12:39,40.

In addition to these more direct sayings, Paul makes numerous indirect allusions to the teachings of Jesus, for example:

1	Practical ethics	Romans 12:9 to 13:10; cf. Matthew Chs 5 to 7.
2	The return of Jesus	1 & 2 Thessalonians; cf. Matthew 24.

It is beyond the scope of this work to enter into details at this point. The interested reader is referred to F.F. Bruce, *Paul, Apostle of the Free Spirit*, pages 100–112. The comments made about the life of the historical Jesus are true here also. First, Paul is able to give information as the need arises. Apparently what is listed above does not exhaust Paul's knowledge of the teachings of Jesus. Second, what we read in Paul of the words of Jesus are confirmed in the gospels. At points where we can check him, Paul proves trustworthy, as the reader will observe as he examines the comparative references.

The historical Jesus: his attributes

The apostle Paul was aware of the personal attributes of the historical Jesus. As need arose, he exhorted his readers to live and act according to the example of Jesus. Let us consider how Paul used the known character of Jesus in his ministry to four groups of readers.

1 The Roman Christians were divided into ethnic groups each of which was divided against the other groups. Paul therefore wrote: "let each of us please his neighbour for his good...For Christ did not please himself..." (Romans 15:2,3).

Paul's reference to the obedient behaviour of Christ (he "did not please himself"), reminds us of the statement of Christ: "I seek not my own will but the will of him who sent me" (John 5:30).

Paul, therefore, told those racially segregated Romans: "Welcome one another, therefore, as Christ has welcomed you" (Romans 15:7).

Christ often used words of welcome, particularly to people in need; for instance: "Come to me...and I will give you rest" (Matthew 11:28).

2 A second group, the Philippians, were behaving proudly in their dealings with one another. Paul encouraged them to "Have this mind among yourselves which is yours in Christ Jesus...he humbled himself..." (Philippians 2:5,8).

Once more we see Paul putting to people the example of Jesus. In the famous invitation "come to me", quoted above, Jesus went on to say: "...I am gentle and lowly in heart." (Matthew 11:29). Paul's "he humbled himself" is from the same Greek word-group as Jesus' disclosure "I am lowly".

3 A third group of readers, the Corinthians, spurned Paul's style of ministry as weak. In reply he states: "I, Paul, myself entreat you, by the meekness and gentleness of Christ..." (2 Corinthians 10:1).

The word "meekness" is basically the same as "gentle", the other word in Matthew 11:29 quoted above. Thus Jesus' words about himself being "gentle" and "lowly", as quoted in Matthew 11:29, are twice drawn upon by Paul, yet in such an inconspicuous way that the point is easily missed.

In his first letter to the Corinthians, Paul urges the readers to "seek" the good of their neighbours, "that they may be saved". Again, Christ is given as the example: "Be imitators of me, as I am of Christ." (1 Corinthians 11:1).

These words remind us of Jesus' important statement to the tax collector, Zacchaeus: "For the Son of man came to seek and to save the lost." (Luke 19:10).

In using the words "seek" and "save", Paul has echoed the sense of purpose which we find in these words of Jesus.

4 The apostle told a fourth group of readers, the Galatians, about the love of Christ, "the Son of God who loved me and gave himself for me" (Galatians 2:20; cf. 2 Corinthians 5:14).

It was the fourth evangelist who drew particular attention to the love of Jesus in his death for sinners. On the evening before the crucifixion Jesus acted out the meaning of love by washing the feet of the disciples. John commented: "having loved his own who were in the world, he loved them to the end" (John 13:1). Had Paul discussed these matters with John at the missionary "summit" in Jerusalem c.47? (cf. Galatians 2:7–9).

While the apostle Paul apparently wrote before the gospels were completed, it is quite possible that in his several visits to Jerusalem he became aware of sources which would in time become part of the finished gospels. Paul displays comprehensive understanding of the character of the historical Jesus—his obedience, his gracious welcome, his meekness and humility, his love for sinners and his desire to save them. Everything Paul affirms about the attributes of Jesus can be confirmed from the gospels.

In speaking of the character of the historical Jesus, however, the apostle is not referring only to a figure of the remote past. The historical Lord is now through death and resurrection the heavenly Lord who has taken his spiritual and emotional personality intact with him to the right hand of the Father. Sometimes Christians find it difficult to imagine what their Lord is like and they do not know how to approach him. The one who is now our heavenly Lord was once the historical Lord. He reacted to suffering with compassion and to injustice with anger. Jesus displayed a wide range of human emotions; and he was both meek and majestic. The point is, as he was, so he is; he is now what he was then. We relate to him now as if we were relating to him then. The heavenly Lord has the same personal attributes as the historical Lord.

So, although primarily interested in Jesus as his contemporary, heavenly Lord, the apostle Paul was by no means unaware of the career of the historical Lord. Through the *paradoseis* or ''traditions'' about Jesus, received from those who had been eyewitnesses of the Lord, Paul supplies information about the birth, life, death, personal attributes and sayings of Christ. Paul's facts, while not extensive, when checked against the gospels, prove to be correct in every case. It is clear that Paul did not manufacture details about Jesus or exaggerate what details he had. Paul's use of historical evidence was, it appears, both careful and sober.

Further reading to Chapter Eleven:

F.F. Bruce, *Paul, Apostle of the Free Spirit*, Paternoster, Exeter, 1977.

W.D. Davies, *Paul and Rabbinic Judaism*, S.P.C.K., London, 1965.

A.M. Hunter, *Paul and His Predecessors*, S.C.M., London, 1961.

S. Kim, *The Origin of Paul's Gospel*, Eerdmans, Grand Rapids, 1981.

Notes

[1] Possibly from AD 48 if Galatians is Paul's first letter.

[2] Galatians 1:19 perhaps refers to an initial, private consultation. *See* Acts 9:27-28 where Paul met a wider group in Jerusalem.

[3] The list of resurrection appearances in 1 Corinthians 15:4-8, suggests that they occurred within a limited period of time.

[4] D.C. Allison, "The Pauline Epistles and the Synoptic Gospels: The Pattern of the Parables", *New Testament Studies*, 28, 1982, pp.1-32.

[5] D.M. Stanley, *The Apostolic Church in the New Testament*, Westminster, Md; Newman, 1967, pp.34-37, 364-369.

CHAPTER TWELVE

The Acts of the Apostles

What is the Book of Acts?

The period of time covered by Luke's second volume is about thirty years (c. 33 to c. 63), the first thirty years of the history of Christianity. But how accurate, how trustworthy is the Book of the Acts of the Apostles in its account of this critical era?

Before answering that question, it is important to establish the following point. Like the gospels, Acts must be understood on its ówn terms. Herein lies the problem. From early times it has been common to require this book to be something it is not.

In the latter half of the second century, for example, there was compiled in Rome a list of New Testament books, with comments on authorship and origin. The Muratorian Canon, named after its modern publisher, Ludovico Muratori, says: "The Acts...of all the Apostles are written in one book". Evidently the fifth book of the New Testament was already known by that name, or something like it, when the Muratorian Canon was written. But how correct was it to designate the book by that title, or even the shorter version by which we now refer to it? Although the names of the apostles are given at the beginning, only one of the twelve, Peter, is involved in the narrative and he virtually fades out of the picture after Chapter Twelve. For the remainder of Acts the spotlight falls on one man, Luke's chief character, the apostle Paul. The author, in fact, did not set out to write about the deeds of *all* the apostles. Therefore the title as it stands is not entirely appropriate.

It is also misleading to regard this book as the history of Christianity for those three decades. Since the author makes no such claim for Acts, it is unreasonable for others to try to force it into this mould. Even allowing for differences between modern and ancient histories, there are too many omissions of vital detail for Acts to be regarded as the first church history. The following examples will be sufficient to demonstrate this.

After Paul, newly converted, arrived in Damascus we read that "for several days he was with the disciples" (Acts 9:19).

A modern historian would investigate who those disciples were and how they came to be at distant Damascus so early in the history of Christianity. A near-contemporary like Josephus might offer some comment, but not Luke. Even more striking is Luke's failure to explain the origins of Christians in Phoenicia (Acts 15:3), Puteoli (Acts 28:14) or Rome (Acts 28:15). One sentence from Luke about the beginnings of Christianity in Rome would have saved hundreds of pages of speculation in the centuries which followed.

A second example of Paul's list of sufferings in 2 Corinthians:

> Five times I have received at the hands of the Jews the forty lashes less one. Three times I have been beaten with rods; once I was stoned. Three times I have been shipwrecked... (2 Corinthians 11:24,25).

Apart from the flogging and imprisonment of Paul in Philippi (Acts 16:22-24), Luke gives no information about those experiences, and yet we do not doubt that they occurred. Such omissions raise serious questions as to whether Luke set out to write a comprehensive history of the first decades of Christianity.

If Acts is not a book about the deeds of the apostles nor the history of the church c.AD 33-63, what is it?

Aim of Acts

I hesitate to add more words to the volumes of opinion about the aims of the author of Acts, especially in a modest book like this. However, in answering the question about Luke's purposes in writing we must look in a straightforward way at his finished product. What do we discover?

As we read, we can discern two closely connected primary emphases.

First, we notice that the story told in Acts begins in Jerusalem and ends in Rome. To the Jew, Jerusalem was the centre, while Rome was the "ends of the earth" (see Acts 1:8; cf. Ps. of Solomon 8:15). To the Gentile, as one suspects Theophilus[1] (Acts 1:1) was, Rome was the hub of the inhabited world. The author recounts how the gospel broke out of Jerusalem into Judaea and from Judaea to Samaria and from Samaria to the Gentiles and ultimately to Rome. In Acts he tells the story, through a series of smaller stories, of the triumphant procession of the preaching of the kingdom from Jerusalem to Rome. In passing we note that the bearer of the message arrived in Rome, not in the triumphant manner of a conquering general, but almost unnoticed as a prisoner in chains; a reverse triumphal entry. (See 2 Corinthians 2:14).

Second, it becomes clear that the author wants us to understand that the bearer of God's word to the Gentiles and to the Gentile world capital was Paul. Certainly Peter is prominent in the early stories, but after the Jerusalem Council (Acts 15:16-11) he does not reappear. Luke shows us first how Peter brought the gospel to the Gentiles (Acts 9:32 to 10:47). Then he shows us how Paul brought the gospel to the Gentiles (beginning Acts 13:1 but see particularly 13:46,47). If Peter, who brought the gospel to the Gentiles was an apostle, then Paul also was an apostle (Acts 14:4,14). There is evidence that sections of the Jewish Christian community were bent on telling the Gentiles that Paul was not a genuine apostle (See 1 Corinthians 9:2, 2 Corinthians 12:12). That Luke describes Christ's call of Paul not once, not twice, but three times (9:1-9; 22:3-21; 26:2-23), shows that the author desired to establish Paul's credentials as the apostle to the Gentiles.

While Luke had lesser aims in writing, these two are, I believe, his main ones. But how does he achieve his objectives? Consider the first chapter. The author could have written:

> Due to the treachery and the death of Judas there was a vacancy in the apostolic company. The Christians met and appointed Matthias to fill the vacancy.[2]

But no. Luke conveys this information by means of a story told in such a way that we can see it in our minds. As we read on we find that Acts is a series of dramatic stories. This is not simply to make his narrative more interesting. There is the deeper intention to "edify" the readers.[3] As in the case of the gospels, the writer is addressing the will and the emotions, not merely the intellect.

The essential character of Acts is expressed in the very first sentence:

> In the first book, O Theophilus, I have dealt with all that Jesus began to do and teach, until the day when he was taken up...

We are meant to understand this to be a second book in which the author deals with all that Jesus will *continue* to do and teach after the day he was taken up. If the opening words anticipate the deeds and teachings of the ascended Jesus, the book as it unfolds by means of connected stories tells how Paul, the "chosen instrument" of the glorified Lord (Acts 9:15), would bring the word of God to the Gentiles and to Rome (Acts 26:16-18).

How trustworthy?

There are four reasons, in particular, which encourage us to have a high regard for the historical trustworthiness of the Acts of the Apostles.

1 Luke's proven use of sources

Paul is the chief character of Acts, with Peter playing an important, but lesser, role. In describing what happened, the author will usually write "Peter...he" or "Paul... he". Where Peter or Paul have companions the plural pronoun "they" is used.

There are three passages, however, when the pronoun "we" is used. This means that the author of Luke–Acts has become part of his narrative, along with Paul and his companions. The three "we" passages are:

Acts 16:10–16	Journey from Troas to Philippi in c.50.
20:5 to 21:17	Journey from Philippi to Jerusalem in c.57.
27:1 to 28:14	Journey from Caesarea to Rome in c.60.

These three passages supply a wealth of information about places, people and time. They are the most detailed passages of the whole of Acts, as one would expect, because the author was an eyewitness of what he describes. Consider, for example, the concentration of historical detail in Luke's account of Paul's journey from Caesarea to Rome in Acts 27:1 to 28:14, the final "we" passage.

Where did the author find the information for the other parts of Acts? Since Luke was a travelling companion of Paul in the "we" passages, we suppose that Paul himself was Luke's source for those other passages which focus on Paul. A substantial part of Acts is taken up with the deeds of Paul—as a persecutor (7:58 to 8:3), as an early convert in Damascus (9:1–30), as a leader in the church in Antioch (11:25–30), as a travelling missionary (12:25 to 28:31).

The remainder of the Acts of the Apostles is devoted to the early Christian community in Jerusalem and the spread of the gospel to other parts of Palestine.

What were Luke's sources of information for these earliest parts of his narrative? Unfortunately he does not

142

identify the people or documents on whom he depended. It is clear, however, that Luke met people who could have supplied the raw material for his book. In the second of the "we" passages, describing the journey from Philippi to Jerusalem, the author met three men who were present in the early days of Christianity in Palestine. At Caesarea Luke met the prophet Agabus (21:10) who was active in the Jerusalem church in the middle forties. Also at Caesarea, Paul and Luke stayed with Philip the Evangelist (21:8) who was a Hellenist Christian from the early thirties and who himself subsequently evangelized the Samaritans and the coastal region from Azotus to Caesarea. On their arrival in Jerusalem Paul and Luke stayed with Mnason, a Cypriot, who had been a disciple from the earliest times (21:16). Luke's contact with Agabus, Philip and Mnason could well have provided considerable information for the narrative that Luke would one day write. Doubtless there were many opportunities for Luke to seek information from other people in Jerusalem and Caesareà during Paul's two year imprisonment in Caesarea. If Peter was in Rome when Luke and Paul arrived in the early sixties, Luke would have had further opportunities to gather information for the story of those early years in Jerusalem.

Fortunately there are two ways in which we can check Luke's accuracy in using sources. One is, as we shall see, the care with which he uses information supplied by the apostle Paul. The other is, as we have already seen, the sober way he handles the text of Mark's gospel, much of which he incorporates within his own. Although we have no means of cross-checking the ways in which we suppose Luke used information from Agabus, Philip and Mnason, his credibility is so strong at the points where he can be checked that we are confident in his integrity at those points where we have no way to check him.

2 Information about Paul in Acts

There is a certain amount of historical information about

Paul to be found in the Acts of the Apostles, most of it in speeches attributed to Paul. Where could Luke have obtained this information except from Paul? The possibility that Luke had access to Paul's letters and gleaned his data from them is fairly unlikely. Paul's letters were not yet gathered into one collection, and in any case, Luke's style and vocabulary show little evidence of being influenced by Paul's letters.

Let us consider the two classes of information about Paul in the Acts of the Apostles which can be checked in his letters. There is first, the cluster of information relating to Paul's conversion and his early life as a Christian. The chief source from Paul is in Galatians, with some amplification in 2 Corinthians and Philippians. The corresponding passages in Acts are the narrative of his conversion in Chapter 9 and the two autobiographical speeches in Chapters 22 and 26 (see pp.144–5).

Paul's confirmation of the Acts information relating to the broad outline of his conversion and early career is striking, the more so, since the author of Acts apparently did not have access to Paul's letters. It would not be true, however, to suggest that there were no problems in the dovetailing of Acts and Paul. Acts, for example, omits any reference to Paul's sojourn in Arabia (see Galatians 1:17). Moreover, Acts attributes the danger in Damascus to the Jews (Acts 9:23) whereas in Paul it is the ethnarch of the Arabian King Aretas from whom Paul escapes (2 Corinthians 11:32,33). According to Acts, Paul went in and out among the apostles in Jerusalem (Acts 9:28) whereas in Galatians, the only apostles with whom Paul conferred were Cephas and James (Galatians 1:18,19). In Acts Paul states that he evangelized throughout all the country of Judaea (Acts 26:19,20), whilst in Galatians 1:22, he writes that he was not known by sight to the churches of Judaea.

It is possible that each and every one of these discrepancies could be harmonized if we possessed more complete documentation. It must always be remembered

	Paul's letters	Acts narrative
HIS "FORMER LIFE IN JUDAISM" (Galatians 1:13)	Are they Israelites? So am I. (2 Corinthians 11:22) As to the law, a Pharisee. (Philippians 3:5)	I am a Jew. (22:3) I have lived as a Pharisee. (26:5)
ZEALOUS PERSECUTOR	As to zeal a persecutor of the church. (Philippians 3:6)	Being zealous for God...I persecuted this Way to the death. (22:3,4)
GOD'S CALL	[God]..called me...was pleased to reveal his Son to me. (Galatians 1:15,16)	At Damascus...he proclaimed Jesus saying "He is the Son of God". (9:19,20)
SENT TO THE GENTILES	[God]..called me...that I might preach [his Son] among the Gentiles. (Galatians 1:15,16)	"I am Jesus...I have appeared...to appoint you...to witness to the things in which you have seen me... the Gentiles—to whom I send you." (26:15–17)

EARLY MINISTRY IN DAMASCUS	At Damascus... I was let down in a basket. (2 Corinthians 11:32,33 cf. Galatians 1:17)	At Damascus...let [Paul] down over the wall, lowering him in a basket. (9:25)
FIRST VISIT TO JERUSALEM	Then after three years I went up to Jerusalem. (Galatians 1:18)	When he had come to Jerusalem. (9:26)
DANGER IN JUDAEA	[The Jews] drove us out [of Judaea]. (1 Thessalonians 2:15)	The Hellenists...were seeking to kill him. (9:29)
WITHDRAWAL TO SYRIA-CILICIA	Then I went into the regions of Syria and Cilicia (Galatians 1:21)	They brought him down to Caesarea and sent him off to Tarsus. (9:30)

that Acts is no more a straight biography of Paul than his own letters are autobiographical. In both Acts and Paul's letters historical details, while important, are secondary and incidental. On the face of it, then, the broad sequence of these early events, as is found in Acts, is confirmed by Paul's letters, whilst there are, at the same time, a number of awkward but minor discrepancies.

The second class of information found in Acts which also appears in Paul's letters concerns four miscellaneous incidents or movements during the subsequent stages of his missionary career. These can be stated briefly.

One relates to what was apparently Paul's second visit as a Christian to Jerusalem, fourteen years after his conversion. Whilst Acts gives the reason for the visit as famine relief (Acts 11:27–30), Paul states that it was to hold a private meeting with James, Peter and John (Galatians 2:1–10). There is no good reason to doubt that both sources are describing the same visit.

Another relates to the incident in Antioch after Paul's return from his missionary tour of Galatia. Both Acts (15:2) and Galatians (2:12,13) refer to a serious dispute between Paul and certain visitors from Jerusalem. Although the two sources give, on the face of it, different grounds for the dispute, there can be little doubt that Galatians 2:11–14 corroborates Acts 15:1,2.

Describing the second missionary tour, Acts narrates Paul's visit to Philippi, Thessalonica, Athens and Corinth along with the movements of his colleagues Timothy and Silas (Acts 16:12; 17:1,15; 18:1,5). Details are corroborated in Paul's first letter to the Thessalonians (2:1,2; 3:1–6 cf.2 Corinthians 1:19).

There was also the journey from Ephesus to Macedonia at the end of the third missionary journey (Acts 20:1), which is confirmed by Paul in the second Corinthian letter (2 Corinthians 2:12,13).

We may say with both classes of data in mind, that although neither author was primarily attempting to write a history, and although there are some "loose ends", in those places where the data overlaps, the details in Paul's letters amply corroborate the broad historicity of the Acts of the Apostles.

We return to our question: Where could Luke have obtained his information about Paul, except from Paul? We have excluded the letters of Paul as the source of data. Paul himself was Luke's source for both kinds of information. As Paul's travelling companion in c.50 and c.57, Luke had ample opportunity to find out about Paul's earlier travelling movements. With regard to the information about Paul's career as a Pharisee and persecutor, followed by his conversion and early ministry, we should note that Luke may well have been present when Paul delivered the speeches in Acts 22 and 26 setting forth the information. Paul's letters, and the historical details they contain, remain an objective measure of the care with which Luke incorporated into Acts the verbal details almost certainly supplied by Paul.

3 External events

The most remarkable external corroboration of the historicity of Acts relates to Paul's ministry in Corinth. When he arrived there he met Aquila and Priscilla who were:

> lately come from Italy...because Claudius had commanded all the Jews to leave Rome (Acts 18:2).

Suetonius, the Roman historian, refers to this event which occurred in Rome c.49:

> Since the Jews constantly made disturbances at the instigation of Chrestus[4] he [Claudius] expelled them from Rome.[5]

Luke and Suetonius unconsciously corroborate each other's accounts.

Aquila and Priscilla must have arrived in Corinth in AD 49 or later. Since Paul came there after them, we may fix AD 49 as the earliest possible time for his arrival in Corinth. As it happens, we are also able to establish the latest possible date for Paul's arrival in Corinth. Earlier this century an inscription was discovered at Delphi in Greece which noted the appointment of Gallio as Proconsul of Achaia (the province of which Corinth was the capital) in July 51.[6] Paul, therefore, must have come to Corinth somewhere between 49 and 51, in all probability late in the year 50. Thus the interlocking pieces of evidence from Suetonius and Delphi exactly confirm Luke's account of Paul's period in Corinth.

The Acts accounts describe Paul standing before the tribunal or *bema* (Acts 18:12), on which Gallio the governor sat conducting the court hearing. Archaeologists have discovered in the forum of Corinth a speaker's platform which is elsewhere referred to as the *rosta*, a Latin word corresponding to the Greek *bema*. It was, doubtless, before this platform that the apostle Paul stood before Gallio in AD 51.

While this is the most extensive pattern of information external to Acts, it is by no means alone. The narrative refers to the high priests Annas (4:6) and Ananias (23:2), Herod Agrippa I (12:1-3, 20,23), Herod Agrippa II (25:13-26:32), Sergius Paulus, proconsul of Cyprus (13:7), the Egyptian prophet (21:38), the procurators Felix (23:23-24:27) and Festus (24:27). Each of these persons is referred to in sources outside the New Testament.

Since Luke proves to be so accurate with these well-known persons, we may reasonably express confidence in his references to lesser persons about whom the major historical sources make no mention—Simon the magician (8:9), the centurion Cornelius (10:1 to 11:18), Antipas' courtier Manaen (13:1), Elymas the magician (13:8), Dionysius the Areopagite (17:34), Demetrius the silversmith (19:24), the tribune Claudius Lysias (23:26), the advocate Tertullus (24:1,2), the centurion Julius (27:1) and Publius the chief man of Malta (28:7). The list of public figures, some major some minor, is impressive.

There can be no doubt that while Acts does not

purport to be *the* history of primitive Christianity, it is nevertheless historical in character.

It would not be true, however, to say there were no problems in Luke's double-volumed work.[7] Two, in particular, deserve mention.

In Gamaliel's speech to the Sanhedrin he states:

Before these days Theudas arose... after him Judas the Galilean arose" (Acts 5:36–37).

"Judas the Galilean" is straightforward. He led an uprising at the changeover of government in Judaea from the Herods to the Romans which occurred in AD 6. The only "Theudas" known to historical records was a prophet who arose c.45, that is, not "before" but "after" Judas. Many accuse Luke of error at this point. Theudas, however, was not an uncommon name and the period before AD 6 was very turbulent, especially after the death of Herod in 4 BC. Indeed, had he placed Theudas after Judas, Luke would be really open to criticism, since Gamaliel's speech occurred about ten years before the Theudas known to historians. As it stands, given Luke's care in other areas where he can be checked and the lack of information about Theudas, it is better to give Luke the benefit of the doubt.

The other and more serious matter is the author's statement about the birth of Jesus:

In those days a decree went out from Caesar Augustus that all the world should be enrolled. This was the first enrolment, when Quirinius was governor of Syria (Luke 2:1,2; cf. Acts 5:37).

The problem is that, according to Josephus (*A.J.* 18:1–2) Quirinius conducted an enrolment in Judaea at the time of the changeover from Herodian to Roman rule in AD 6. But Matthew (2:1) as well as Luke himself (1:5–28) place the birth of Jesus in the days of Herod the Great, who died in 4 BC. On the face of it, Luke 2:1–2 is astray by approximately ten years. While the words "first enrolment" may be taken to refer to an enrolment prior

to the more famous occurrence of AD 6, complete and
continuous records of governors in Syria leave no room
for Quirinius to have been governor at an earlier date.
Many scholars have seized on this verse as evidence of
Luke's inaccuracy in historical matters. This is hardly
fair. In the Greek original so few words are used that it
can be translated in several ways. The version,

> This was an *earlier* enrolment, *before* Quirinius was
> governor of Syria.

is less attractive grammatically, but is quite consistent
historically with Luke's own fixing of the birth of Jesus in
the days of Herod. There is good reason to leave this
question open pending the availability of more evidence
before sweepingly rejecting Luke's competence as a
historian.

The problems in Luke must be kept in proper perspective. The areas of serious difficulty are limited to two or
three which are, in each case, highly complex. On the
other hand, on the numerous occasions where Luke has
committed himself to specific details he can be shown to
be accurate. The great archaeologist Sir William Ramsay
once commented that "Luke's history is unsurpassed in
respect of its trustworthiness".[9]

4 The trivia of Acts

Much of Paul's work, as recorded in Acts, occurred in the
Roman provinces of Cyprus, Galatia, Asia, Macedonia
and Achaia. After they conquered a region, the Romans
wisely allowed local methods of government to continue
for a period. Writing of the era in which Acts describes
Paul's labours, E.A. Judge comments:

> The standardization of government had by no means
> worked itself out, nor was Roman control yet evenly
> imposed in every quarter. The Acts of the Apostles is
> a kaleidoscope of local diversity.[10]

The eminent Roman historian A.N. Sherwin-White
has examined incidental references in the Acts to trials,
punishment, city government and citizenship. In case

after case he finds that the "narrative agrees with the evidence of the earlier period". In summary, Sherwin-White states about the Acts:

Any attempt to reject its basic historicity even in matters of detail must now appear absurd.[11]

Acts indeed captures the sense of local diversity referred to above, as three examples will demonstrate. In Thessalonica the decisions about Paul were made by "the Politarchs" (Acts 17:8), a word which appears rarely in ancient books. The inscription over the archway of the Vandar Gate at Thessalonica, now in the British Museum, reads "In the time of the Politarchs", thus demonstrating Luke's accurate attention to detail. Similarly, in the account of the riot in Ephesus, capital of Asia, Luke refers to "the Asiarchs" who begged Paul not to enter the theatre (Acts 19:31). Strabo, who wrote about the geography of the times, referred to "the Asiarchs...the first men of their province" (14.1.42). Finally, on the island of Malta Luke's reference to "the chief man of the island, Publius" (Acts 28:7) is confirmed by an inscription which runs "Pudens, equite of the Romans, chief man of Malta" (*I.G.* 14. 601). Space prevents the citation of more evidence, but enough has been presented to make the point that Luke carefully preserves the detailed accuracy of local customs of government.

The answer to the question "How trustworthy is the Acts of the Apostles?" is "Very trustworthy"—provided we don't try to force the book into moulds of our own making rather than Luke's. The book does not set out to narrate what all the apostles did nor is it a comprehensive account of earliest church history. What Luke sets out to show us, in an edifying and not merely informative way, is how the word of God came from the Jewish capital Jerusalem to the Gentile capital Rome, thus vindicating its bearer Paul as the apostle to the Gentiles. Let us read what two scholars have written. They approach their study of Acts from different directions.

C.J. Hemer, in a painstaking study of what he calls "the trivia of Acts", comments:

> I have an interest here in the unimportant, in the nuances, which might betray a redactor's faulty knowledge of the context of a precise but unimportant statement. I submit that it is exceedingly hard to reproduce secondhand, in one's own style, intricate reports of fact. Yet we can check the trivia of Acts against the inscriptions: "town clerk" at Ephesus, "politarchs" at Thessalonica, "first man" of Malta... Less obvious but more pervasive are the marginal things, the incidence of personal names, the illustrations of customs in verbal uses... And there is the factor of the suble interlocking of pieces...the dates of the Gallio inscription...the expulsion of the Jews from Italy... There are in fact incidentals...which contribute unemphatically to the building of a picture which correlates with external literature and with archaeology.[12]

M. Hengel, on the other hand, has compared Acts with other "histories" written at that time. He notices that Luke, like other historians of antiquity, sometimes abbreviates, omits, elaborates or repeats when he writes. Hengel notes:

> All this can be found in the secular histories of Greek and Roman antiquity. On the other hand, one can hardly accuse him of simply having invented events, created scenes out of nothing and depicted them on a broad canvas, deliberately falsifying his traditions in an unrestrained way for the sake of cheap effect. He is quite certainly not simply concerned with pious edification at the expense of truth. He is not just an "edifying writer", but a historian and theologian who needs to be taken seriously. His account always remains within the limits of what was considered reliable by the standards of antiquity.[13]

Is Acts historically trustworthy? Its attention to detail, as well as its observable style relative to that of other ancient histories, suggests that the answer is in the affirmative.

Further reading to Chapter Twelve:
M. Hengel, *Acts and the History of Earliest Christianity*, E.T. S.C.M., London, 1979.
I.H. Marshall, *Luke: Historian and Theologian*, Paternoster, Exeter, 1970.
W.M. Ramsay, *St. Paul the Traveller and Roman Citizen*, Baker, Michigan, 1960.
A.N.Sherwin-White, *Roman Society and Roman Law in the New Testament*, O.U.P., London, 1965.

Notes
[1]Acts is addressed to "Theophilus" but it is not clear whether he was a real or symbolic person.

[2]*See* W. Barclay, *The Gospels and Acts*, Vol.2, S.C.M., London, 1976, p.229.

[3]E. Haenchen, *The Acts of the Apostles*, E.T. 1971, p.103 refers to Luke–Acts as "a book of edification"

[4]A misspelling of Christus.

[5]*Life of Claudius* 25:1.

[6]J. Finegan, *The Archaeology of the New Testament*, Boulder, 1981, p.12.

[7]For a summary of the problems of history in Acts *see* W. Barclay, *The Gospel and Acts*, vol.2, pp.259–281.

[8]*See* F.F. Bruce, *The Acts of the Apostles*, Tyndale, London, 1965, p.147.

[9]Quoted in F.F. Bruce, *The New Testament Documents*, IVP, Leicester, 1979, p.90.

[10]*Reformed Theological Review* XXX, 1971, p.7.

154

[11]*Roman Society and Roman Law in the New Testament*, O.U.P., Oxford, 1965.

[12]"Luke the Historian" in *Bulletin of the John Rylands Library*, No.60, pp.36,37.

[13]M. Hengel, *Acts and the History of Earliest Christianity*, E.T., London, 1979, p.61.

CHAPTER THIRTEEN

Is the New Testament Historically Reliable?

Let us draw together the threads of the argument.

The aim of this book has been to examine the historical reliability of the New Testament. Most people want to know whether or not the New Testament is historically true before they can begin to think about believing its theological message. If they doubt the historical truth of the New Testament, that is the end of the matter.

We have not, therefore, asked the reader to accept that New Testament documents are special in any religious way. The question of historical reliability can be discussed apart from the question of "inspiration" and that is what we have done.

Many readers will have been surprised to learn how much the gospels, Acts and the autobiographical parts of Paul's letters have in common with ancient history writers like Thucydides or Josephus. Few, if any, of the history writers of antiquity wrote "pure" history to provide the reader with "mere" facts. Facts were presented, certainly, but to make a point.

Thucydides, for example, wrote to provide "an exact knowledge of the past" which, he continued, would act "as an aid to the interpretation of the future".[1]

Thucydides provided a factual account but he had an underlying motive for writing.

The historian Josephus (37–96?) was, like most of the New Testament writers, a Jew, and moreover, one whose life span overlapped Paul's. In the opening lines of the *Jewish War* Josephus stated his commitment to factual narration: "I...propose to provide the subjects of the Roman Empire with a narrative of the facts" (1:3). His deeper intentions, however, may be discerned in the words:

> In my reflections on the events I cannot conceal my private sentiments...my country...owed its ruin to civil strife... it was the Jewish tyrants who drew down upon the holy temple the unwilling hands of the Romans (1:10).

What makes Josephus so interesting is his undoubted ability to provide detailed and factual information, at the same time presenting the readers with a sustained "case" against the revolutionaries among his fellow countrymen. Josephus' historical works greatly add to our knowledge of the Jewish people in the century in which Jesus lived and the early church was born.

This concern for facts, while at the same time making a point, may be discerned also in the gospel writers, explicitly so in the cases of John and Luke. John, for example, stated with reference to the crucifixion, but in a manner which is true of this entire gospel, that:

> He who saw it has borne witness—his testimony is true, and he knows that he tells the truth—that you also may believe. (John 19:35 cf. 21:24; 20:31)

John witnessed to "the truth" so that the reader (20:31) may "believe".

For his part, Luke stated:

> It seemed good to me also, having followed all these things closely [accurately?] for some time past, to write an orderly account for you...that you may know the truth concerning the things of which you have been informed. (Luke 1:3,4)

Luke researched the sources and wrote an orderly, chronologically accurate narrative, so that the reader might know that what Luke learned about Jesus, perhaps by word of mouth, is historically true. It will be remembered that these words of Luke's form an introduction to both his gospel and the Acts of the Apostles.

The writers of the gospels and Acts were people of their own times, as we are of ours. While the gospels and Acts have many distinctive and innovative features they are, in broad terms, recognizable as examples of the history writing of their period. It is both unhelpful and untrue to regard them merely as religious or theological works. They are also unmistakably historical in character. As historical sources for the period, the gospels are as valuable to the general historian as Josephus, except that unlike Josephus they are focused on one person and for a brief period. The eminent Roman historian A.N. Sherwin-White, for example, writes of our dependence on the parables of Jesus for an understanding of life in Galilee at that time:

> The pattern of life, both social and economic, civil and religious, is precisely what is to be expected in the isolated district of Galilee...the absence of Graeco-Roman colouring is a convincing feature of the Galilean narrative and parables.[2]

Sherwin-White goes on to say that "the narrative... coheres beautifully".

The gospels and Acts, therefore, take their place as historical documents which arose from, and also illustrate, a particular period.

We have claimed that Christian sources are as valuable as non-Christian sources for our knowledge of history. Can that be demonstrated? Let us investigate the seventy year period (6 BC–AD 60) which encompasses the life of Jesus and the first generation of his followers. It will be noticed from what follows that there are a number of points at which Christian and non-Christian sources "intersect". For example, both sets of sources indicate that Archelaus succeeded Herod as ruler of Judaea and, that subsequently, when Quirinius was governor of Syria the people of Judaea were subjected to a form of personal taxation levied by the Romans.

As you compare the two sets of information you will notice that the Christian sources are as detailed and careful as the non-Christian sources. Christian sources contribute, on an equal footing with non-Christian sources, pieces of information which form part of the fabric of known history. In matters of historical detail, the Christian writers are as valuable to the historian as the non-Christian.

What is the point of these comparisons? Just this: if at the point of "intersection" the Christian evidence about kings, governors and other important people is proved reliable by the non-Christian evidence, should we not also accept Christian evidence about lesser persons as reliable even though there is no "intersecting" non-Christian evidence? To be consistent we will be prepared to accept Jairus, Joseph of Arimathaea and Nicodemus, to mention just three, as genuine figures of history although, through lack of notoriety or fame, they were unrecorded in secular sources.

Intersections

6 BC	King Herod and the killing of the boys	Then Herod...sent and killed all the male children in Bethlehem and in all that region who were two years old or under.... Matthew (2:16)	When [Augustus] heard that Herod king of the Jews had ordered all the boys in Syria under the age of two to be put to death and that the king's son was among those killed, he said "I'd rather be Herod's pig than Herod's son". (Macrobius, *Saturnalia* 2:4:11)
4 BC	Archelaus ruler of Judaea	...when he [Joseph] heard that Archelaus reigned over Judea in place of his father Herod.... (Matthew 2:22)	[Augustus] gave half the kingdom to Archelaus with the title of ethnarch. (Josephus *Jewish War* 2:94)
AD 6,7	Roman Annexation and Assessment	the...enrolment, when Quirinius was governor of Syria ... (Luke 2:2)	The territory subject to Archelaus was added to Syria, and Quirinius...was sent by Caesar to take a census of property in Syria and to sell the Estate of Archelaus. (Josephus *Jewish Antiquities* 17:355)
AD 6,7	The revolt of Judas	...Judas the Galilean arose in the days of the census... (Acts 5:37)	The territory of Archelaus was now reduced to a province...a Galilean...Judas incited his countrymen to revolt...[over] paying tribute to the Romans. (*Jewish War* 2:118)

AD 28	Emperor Prefect High Priest	In the fifteenth year...of Tiberius Caesar, Pontius Pilate being governor of Judea...in the high-priesthood of Annas and Caiaphas, the word of God came to John... (Luke, 3:1,2)	Pilate being sent by Tiberius as procurator to Judaea... (*Jewish War* 2:169) Herod put [John the Baptist] to death, though he was a good man. (*Jewish Antiquities* 18:113–117)
AD 33	Execution of Jesus	So Pilate...delivered him [Jesus] to be crucified. (Mark 15:15)	Christus...suffered the extreme penalty...at the hands of... Pontius Pilate. (Tacitus, *Annals* 15:44)
AD c.36	Aretas IV (9 BC–AD 40) king of the Nabateans	At Damascus, the governor under King Aretas guarded the city of Damascus in order to seize me... (2 Corinthians 11:32)	A quarrel...arose between Aretas king of Petra, and Herod [Antipas] [who] had taken the daughter of Aretas as his wife. (*Jewish Antiquities* 18:109)
AD 44	Death of Agrippa I	...the people of Tyre and Sidon ...come to him in a body... asked for peace... Herod put on his royal robes, took his seat upon the throne and made an oration to them. And the people shouted "The voice of a god, and not of a man!" Immediately an angel of the Lord smote him, because he did not give God the glory... (Acts 12:20–23)	Clad in a garment woven completely of silver...he entered the theatre at day-break. There the silver, illuminated by the touch of the first rays of the sun... inspired awe...his flatterers addressed him as a god...the king did not rebuke him...felt a stab of pain in his heart...after five days...he departed this life. (*Jewish Antiquities* 19:344–349)

AD 45, 46	Famine	Agabus...foretold...a great famine over all the world; and this took place in the days of Claudius. (Acts 11:28)	It was in the administration of Tiberius Alexander that the great famine occurred in Judaea. (Jewish Antiquities 20:101)
AD 49	Claudius' expulsion of Jews from Rome	to Corinth...And he [Paul] found a Jew named Aquila, a native of Pontus, lately come from Italy with his wife Priscilla, because Claudius had commanded all the Jews to leave Rome. (Acts 18:2)	Since the Jews constantly made disturbances at the instigation of Chrestus, he [Claudius] expelled them from Rome. (Suetonius, Life of Claudius 25:4)
AD 51	Gallio, proconsul of Achaia	But when Gallio was proconsul of Achaia... (Acts 18:12)	See the inscription at Delphi which fixed Gallio's appointment at (July) c.AD 51.
c.AD 57	James the brother of Jesus	When we had come to Jerusalem ...Paul went in with us to James; and all the elders were present. (Acts 21:17,18)	c.AD 62 Death of Festus...Caesar sent Albinus...The king removed Joseph from high priesthood... bestowed the succession on the son of Ananus, likewise called the ...Ananus...convened the judges of the Sanhedrin and brought before them...James, the brother of Jesus who was called the Christ...to be stoned. (Jewish Antiquities 20:200)

c.AD 57 The Egyptian Prophet	Are you not the Egyptian, then, who recently stirred up a revolt and led the four thousand men of the Assassins out into the wilderness? (Acts 21:38)	The Egyptian false prophet... appeared in the country, collected a following of about thirty thousand dupes, and led them... from the desert to the... mount of Olives. (*Jewish War* 2:261)
c.AD 47 Ananias the high priest	And the High Priest Ananias commanded those who stood by him to strike him [Paul] on the mouth. (Acts 23:2; cf. 24:1)	Herod King of Chalcis now removed Joseph, the son of Camei, from the High Priesthood and assigned the office to Ananias, son of Nebedaios, as successor. (*Jewish Antiquities* 20:103)
c.AD 52 Felix, Roman procurator (AD 52–60) and Drusilla	...Felix...with his wife Drusilla, who was a Jewess...sent for Paul and heard him speak upon faith in Christ Jesus. (Acts 24:24)	At the time when Felix was procurator of Judaea [Drusilla]... marr[ied] Felix. (*Jewish Antiquities* 20:131–143; cf. Tacitus *History* 5:9 *Annals* 12:54)
c.AD 60 Festus, Roman procurator (AD 60–62?)	But when two years had elapsed, Felix was succeeded by Porcius Festus. (Acts 24:27)	When Porcius Festus was sent by Nero as successor to Felix. (*Jewish Antiquities* 20:182)

King Agrippa II and Berenice

Now, when some days had passed, Agrippa the king and Bernice arrived at Caesarea to welcome Festus. (Acts 25:13)

After the death of Herod [King of Chalcis] who had been her uncle and husband, Bernice lived for a long time as a widow. But when the report gained currency that she had a liaison with her brother [Agrippa] she induced Polemo king of Cilicia to be circumcised and to take her in marriage.... (*Jewish Antiquities* 20:145)

How can we be sure of the historicity of an event or person in antiquity? One historical source may be sufficient to inspire confidence, especially if, at points where he can be checked, the writer proves trustworthy. But if we have more than one source, and if they are independent of each other, the ground becomes even firmer.

History textbooks tell us that a major war occurred in Palestine AD 66–70 between the Jews and the Romans. But did it in fact happen? How do the authors of the textbooks know? How can we know?

We have in Josephus' *Jewish War* a major and detailed written history of the conflict. But in addition we have some information from Tacitus (AD 55–c.120) Suetonius (AD 69–c.140) Dio Cassius (AD 150 to early third century). There are also some coins minted by the Jewish revolutionaries, as well as the archaeological finds at Masada where one of the factions underwent Roman siege. Certainly there are some "loose ends", some discrepancies—that is the nature of primary sources—but there can be no doubt that the war took place.

Similarly, how can we know that Jesus of Nazareth was a genuine figure of history? The method of enquiry is exactly the same in principle as for establishing the reality of the Jewish War. In the case of Jesus we have not one source but many. Most, to be sure, are favourable, but some are neutral, while others are hostile.

Let us summarize some of the ways in which we are able objectively to cross-check historical data from source to source with respect to Jesus and Christian origins.

1 Non-Christian writers like Pliny, Tacitus and Josephus tell us that Jesus was an historical figure who was executed in Judaea sometime between AD 26 and 36, that he was subsequently worshipped as a deity and that the Christian movement spread to many places including to Rome by AD 50 or earlier.

2 The data in the Acts and Paul's letters when cross-

checked against political inscriptions and other sources indicate that Paul's letters were written in the period AD 50–65. These dates are certainly accurate to within a year or two of this time-frame.

3 Leaders of the early Church like Clement, Ignatius, and Polycarp, who wrote late in the first and early in the second centuries, quote extensively from almost every New Testament scroll, thus establishing their existence and use by c.100 at the latest. Paul's letters are obviously much earlier and perhaps other parts are as well. The literature of the New Testament was written closer in time to Jesus than many ancient writings are to the events or persons they describe.

4 The rapid spread of Christianity throughout the Greek-speaking world and from there to Latin, Syriac, and Coptic-speaking areas together with the accompanying need for manuscripts for reading in church and the survival of many of these manuscripts means that today we are able scientifically to reconstruct, almost to perfection, the text of the scrolls of the New Testament as they were originally written.

5 The existence of not one but four gospels gives us many opportunities to cross-check many of the details about Jesus, the focus figure. For two of the writers, Mark and John, eyewitness claims are made and we have attempted to show the reasonableness of those claims. The other two, Matthew and Luke, incorporate Mark within their gospels, a fact which allows us to check their accuracy or their proneness to exaggerate. While neither author slavishly follows Mark, both emerge as sober and careful scribes.

By cross-checking independent author against independent author we can be confident of the details and circumstances of Jesus' birth, the broad outlines and nature of his activities in Galilee and Judaea, the circumstances of his betrayal and execution, as well as those of his resurrection. However, only in a broad sense can a "life of Jesus" be reconstructed from the sources because they are gospels, not biographies in the modern sense. They were each written to present and proclaim Jesus not to become objects of historical research. That they are such, and this to a significant degree, is incidental to their primary function.

6. Luke–Acts and John, which were written independently, both refer to the historic coming of the Holy Spirit soon after the ministry of Jesus. John's gospel is written in such a way as to presume this event (e.g. John 7:39) whereas Luke wrote specifically to describe when and how it happened (Acts 2:1-4; 11:16,17).

7 Paul's letters and the Acts of the Apostles, which were also written independently, are open to cross-checking at a number of points. By this means we can be confident of the existence and the leadership of the Jerusalem church (Acts 1-7; Galatians 1:18-2:9). The same sources, when cross-checked, establish the historic spread of Christianity to the Gentile world, including Rome itself (Acts 28:16; Philippians 1:13; 4:22), a point which Tacitus also corroborates (*Annals* 15.44:2-8).

At many points of historical importance about Jesus and Christian beginnings we have not one but several independent sources, not all of them sympathetic to Jesus. If we accept the historicity of the *Jewish War* on the grounds of independent sources which are able to be cross-checked it is inconsistent to doubt the essential historicity of Jesus and the early church.

Further reading to Chapter Thirteen:
I.H. Marshall, *I Believe in the Historical Jesus*, Hodder &
Stoughton, London, 1976.
J.A.T. Robinson, *Can we trust the New Testament?*
Mowbray, London, 1977.

Notes
[1]*Peloponnesian War*, 1.23.

[2]*Roman Society and Roman Law in the New Testament*, Oxford University Press, Oxford, 1965, pp.138,139.

CHAPTER FOURTEEN

Who Is Jesus?

Whatever your opinion of Jesus there is little doubt that you will have some knowledge of who he was and what happened to him. It is remarkable that he has had, and continues to have, such an impact on people and on history. Unlike ben Kosiba, who died a century later and to whom we have referred already, Jesus wrote no letters, led no armies, minted no coins, issued no land deeds. Yet few have heard of ben Kosiba, whereas Jesus is well-known. Why?

Ben Kosiba enjoyed a tremendous following for his three or so years. More than half a million men were prepared to die for the cause he led, including the pathetic remnants of his forces whom the Romans starved to death in the caves of the bleak desert ravines near the Dead Sea. Such was their loyalty to him that his various letters were carefully bound together and buried in the cave for safekeeping, only to be recovered in the twentieth century. And yet he is as obscure a figure to us as Judas the Galilean, Barabbas or Simon bar Gioras to mention only a few of the dozen spectacular revolutionary leaders who arose in that general period, but who are forgotten today.

Jesus continues to exercise a strange fascination even to many outside the circle of Christian belief and church membership. Movies continue to be made about him, rock operas composed, and outlandish alternative theories put forward.

This is not to imply that Jesus was obscure then, only to become famous later—a kind of reverse ben Kosiba. Jesus had a tremendous impact on events and people in his own generation; the New Testament, whose trustworthiness is the subject of this book, is the tangible evidence of that impact. It is well to remember that the New Testament is not one document, but twenty-seven separate pieces of literature written by nine or ten different authors, most of whom wrote without reference to, or knowledge of what the others had written.

By contrast, it does not seem that even one person felt moved to write abut ben Kosiba immediately after his death,[1] although during his lifetime Rabbi Akiba had hailed him as Messiah, the fulfilment of the long expected star of Jacob who would rule the world (Numbers 24:17). It is for this reason that he was known by some as bar Kokhba, which means son of a star, or Messiah. For others, however, he came to have a different name. After his death, when so many hopes and dreams were smashed, his name was subtly altered by some to ben Koziba, "son of a liar". Notice the sequence—ben Kosiba, bar Kokhba, ben Koziba, oblivion.

Not so with Jesus. Within a few years of his lifetime, nine or ten independent writers had recorded their testimony for all to read. This is to state the numbers conservatively since, as we have seen, buried within Matthew and Luke are the written (or oral) sources Q, L, M and perhaps others as well. Thus we have a dozen independent writers, each of whom presents the same exalted view of Jesus. In a criminal trial such a unity of independent testimony would certainly persuade a judge and jury that what is said is the truth. For my part this analogy holds good for the writers and source-strands which make up the New Testament.

But why did ben Kosiba pass out of memory whereas Jesus created such an impact? It was, in part, that ben

Kosiba failed to defeat the Romans. Further, his period in public life was brief. Oblivion, or relative oblivion, was to be his lot. And the reason? After ben Kosiba died, memory of him died with those who knew him.

Jesus, however, lived on in the memory of his generation and in each generation after. This was not because of his ethical teachings or his reformist insights into contemporary Jewish society. If this had been all there was to it, Jesus would scarcely have survived a century or two in the memories of those who came after him. Ethics and the principles for the reform of society were present in what Jesus said and did; but they are not at the centre. Reduced to the barest essentials, Jesus' "message" was that God himself would soon come into human affairs and establish his kingdom of justice, goodness and peace and that God was already doing this in Jesus' own person. As the Son of God, Jesus was at that very time as well as at the end, the bearer of the kingdom of God in a world corrupted by forces opposite to God's character and purpose. These startling claims of Jesus (imagine if someone said them today) were by no means empty. Demons were cast out, the deaf given their hearing, the blind their sight, the dumb their speech, the sick their health, and the dead their life as visible "signs" of the truth of Jesus' words that the kingdom was and would be present in him. The great and crowning sign that Jesus spoke the truth was that God raised him to life on the third day after his execution by the Romans.

Put simply, the reason Jesus lived and lives subjectively in the memory of his followers is that he lived and lives *objectively* after three days in the tomb. What Jesus said about God's intentions for mankind and what he said about himself as the one who carried out those intentions as God's Son, is confirmed and established by his resurrection from the dead.

Without the resurrection, Jesus becomes just another prophet whose prophecies came to nothing, another mistaken dreamer, another idealistic reformer. And this indeed is all Jesus was, if the resurrection did not take place.

That Jesus can never be viewed primarily as a teacher of ethics or as a reformer of society is quite clear from Paul's words,

> If for this life only we have hoped in Christ, we [Christians] are of all men most to be pitied (1 Corinthians 15:19).

Paul continues immediately, "But in fact Christ has been raised from the dead", something he and his fellow New Testament writers repeatedly say and universally assume.

The resurrection is inextricably part of the fabric of the New Testament; destroy it or remove it and the New Testament becomes an unreliable bundle of rags and tatters.

It is not the purpose of this book to list the evidence for the resurrection. Many others have done that, and with far greater skill. What I am attempting to establish is that a Jesus who died (c.33), as no more than a teacher and reformer, would have been as little known, or almost as little known, as a ben Kosiba who died a century later.

Consider some words of the apostle Paul written to a group of people in far away Macedonia no more than seventeen years after the execution of Jesus:

> You turned to God from idols, to serve a living and true God, and to wait for his Son from heaven, whom he raised from the dead (1 Thessalonians 1.9-10).

Fundamental to what Paul told the Thessalonians was that Jesus was God's Son and that God had raised him from the dead. The active receiving of these pieces of information established the Thessalonians as Christian believers.

Now the question is: was Paul's communication to them true or false? If it was false, Paul was either himself somehow deceived or he was a deliberate deceiver of others. Few people reading Paul would accept the latter view, though the former is certainly possible. But to return to the courtroom analogy, Paul is only one of the witnesses—one witness among a dozen or so. If all the witnesses, independently of each other, state that Jesus was the Son of God and that he was raised from the dead, aṣ they do, what then? I can only ask the reader to be a member of the jury and arrive at his own verdict. For my part the evidence is inescapable.

The logic is simple enough. People became Christians then on the basis of information which they were given about Jesus. The only real questions are: was the information true or untrue? Did the information correspond with, and give expression to, reality or not? The information is an *effect* for which there was a *cause*, like a ripple caused by a stone thrown into a pond. What *caused* the *effect*? Was it the stone thrown into the pond as the bystanders said, or was it something else? Was Jesus in reality the Son of God raised from the dead, as the witnesses said, or were these only words which had no basis in fact? But if what purports to be the cause—the deity and resurrection of Jesus—was not the cause, what was? The writers must all have been either deceived or cold-blooded deceivers.

Those are the questions which I have turned over and over in my mind and looked at from many different angles. Philosophically and scientifically there are problems with a resurrection, and I feel those as keenly as most. But I cannot escape the historical question. Did the resurrection happen or not? If it happened it happened—and so much the worse for my dogmas. I certainly will not be able to regard Jesus with the indifference with which I might view a ben Kosiba. But at that point the questions about Jesus stop, or at least slow down, and the questions about me begin.

Further reading to Chapter Fourteen:
W.L. Craig, "The Empty Tomb of Jesus" in *Gospel Perspectives* II, R.T. France & D. Wenham (eds),

J.S.O.T. Press, Sheffield, 1981.

G.E. Ladd, *I believe in the Resurrection of Jesus*, Hodder & Stoughton, London, 1975.

C.F.D. Moule, *The Phenomenon of the New Testament*, S.C.M. London, 1968.

Notes
[1]Unless whatever was written has been lost.